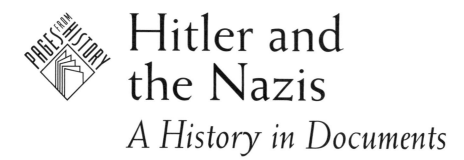

Hitler and the Nazis

A History in Documents

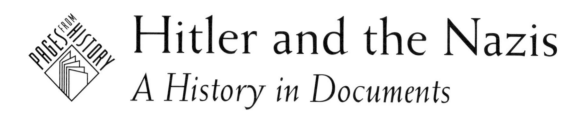

Hitler and the Nazis
A History in Documents

David F. Crew

OXFORD
UNIVERSITY PRESS

For Sara, Kate, Charlotte, and Gabriel

General Editors

Sarah Deutsch
Professor of History
University of Arizona

Carol Karlsen
Professor of History
University of Michigan

Robert G. Moeller
Professor of History
University of California, Irvine

Jeffrey N. Wasserstrom
Professor of History
Indiana University

Board of Advisors

Steven Goldberg
Social Studies Supervisor
New Rochelle, N.Y. Public Schools

John Pyne
Social Studies Supervisor
West Milford, N.J. Public Schools

Oxford University Press, Inc., publishes works that further
Oxford University's objective of excellence
in research, scholarship, and education.

Oxford   New York
Auckland   Cape Town   Dar es Salaam   Hong Kong   Karachi
Kuala Lumpur   Madrid   Melbourne   Mexico City   Nairobi
New Delhi   Shanghai   Taipei   Toronto

With offices in
Argentina   Austria   Brazil   Chile   Czech Republic   France   Greece
Guatemala   Hungary   Italy   Japan Poland   Portugal   Singapore
South Korea   Switzerland   Thailand   Turkey   Ukraine   Vietnam

Copyright © 2005 by David F. Crew

Published by Oxford University Press, Inc.
198 Madison Avenue, New York, New York 10016
www.oup.com

Oxford is a registered trademark of Oxford University Press

Library of Congress Cataloging-in-Publication Data
Crew, David F.
Hitler and the Nazis : a history in documents / David F. Crew.
p. cm.
Includes index.
ISBN-10: 0-19-515285-9
ISBN-13: 978-0-19-515285-2
1. National socialism—History—Sources. 2. Hitler, Adolf, 1889-1945—
Sources. 3. Germany—History—1918-1933—Sources. 4. Germany—
History—1933-1945—Sources. I. Title.
DD253.C67 2005
943.086—dc22

2005017759

Printed in the United States of America
On acid-free paper

Cover: *Adolf Hitler, 1938.*
Frontispiece: *Adolf Hitler, 1935.*
Title page: *Hitler and Heinrich Himmler, 1935.*

Contents

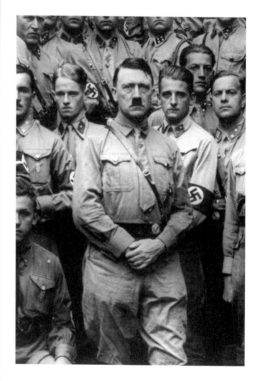

What Is a Document?

To the historian, a document is, quite simply, any sort of historical evidence. It is a primary source, the raw material of history. A document may be more than the expected government paperwork, such as a treaty or passport. It is also a letter, diary, will, grocery list, newspaper article, recipe, memoir, oral history, school yearbook, map, chart, architectural plan, poster, musical score, play script, novel, political cartoon, painting, photograph—even an object.

Using primary sources allows us not just to read about history, but to read history itself. It allows us to immerse ourselves in the look and feel of an era gone by, to understand its people and their language, whether verbal or visual. And it allows us to take an active, hands-on role in (re)constructing history.

Using primary sources requires us to use our powers of detection to ferret out the relevant facts and to draw conclusions from them; just as Agatha Christie uses the scores in a bridge game to determine the identity of a murderer, the historian uses facts from a variety of sources—some, perhaps, seemingly inconsequential—to build a historical case.

The poet W. H. Auden wrote that history was the study of questions. Primary sources force us to ask questions—and then, by answering them, to construct a narrative or an argument that makes sense to us. Moreover, as we draw on the many sources from "the dust-bin of history," we can endow that narrative with character, personality, and texture—all the elements that make history so endlessly intriguing.

Cartoon
This political cartoon addresses the issue of church and state. It illustrates the Supreme Court's role in balancing the demands of the 1st Amendment of the Constitution and the desires of the religious population.

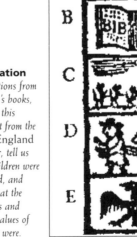

Illustration
Illustrations from children's books, such as this alphabet from the New England Primer, tell us how children were educated, and also what the religious and moral values of the time were.

Treaty

A government document such as this 1805 treaty can reveal not only the details of government policy, but information about the people who signed it. Here, the Indians' names were written in English transliteration by U.S. officials; the Indians added pictographs to the right of their names.

Map

A 1788 British map of India shows the region prior to British colonization, an indication of the kingdoms and provinces whose ethnic divisions would resurface later in India's history.

Literature

The first written version of the Old English epic Beowulf, from the late 10th century, is physical evidence of the transition from oral to written history. Charred by fire, it is also a physical record of the wear and tear of history.

How to Read a Document

Our most extensive source of documentary evidence about Hitler and the Nazis is the Nazis themselves. The Nazis produced huge numbers of documents, including detailed records of their own horrific crimes. Primary sources include speeches, internal Nazi party documents, government records, letters, diaries, and memoirs. As with documents from any period of history, those that help tell the story of Hitler and the Nazis must be considered within their historical context. Factors include the document's author, the date it was written, and under what circumstances, why it was written and the intended audience. Dates, for example, can be particularly important. After World War II, many Germans wanted to clear themselves of any crimes that might have sent them to jail. Therefore, a description of a mass shooting by a participant or observer given as evidence in a post–1945 war crimes trial, may display remorse and guilt that the author did not feel at the time of the event.

However, even the documents produced by the Nazis during their twelve-year dictatorship are often not totally transparent. The Nazis seldom described their attempt to annihilate millions of European Jews as what it was—mass murder. Instead, they used euphemisms such as "The Final Solution" to cover up their crimes. Because of the biases built into Nazi language, it is important to draw upon other sources, such as the reports filed by foreign embassies and news agencies or the diaries, memoirs, and oral histories of surviving victims.

Political Posters
In an era before television, when even radio was still in its infancy, political messages were often communicated to voters by arresting images printed on posters displayed in public spaces.

Delivering the Message
Although posters frequently included written messages, they relied heavily upon their visual impact. With just a few words of text: "Our Last Hope" and Hitler's name, this Nazi election poster from 1932 is a particularly good example. The poster delivers a message that is carried through the visual impact of the many somber faces of desperate unemployed voters.

Audience
Nazi election posters had to compete for the attention of voters with the posters of many other political parties. In this particular case, the Nazis were appealing to the hopelessness felt by the unemployed who would usually have voted for the radical left-wing Communist Party.

Reasons for Taking Photos
Photographs taken by the Nazis recorded a version of reality, but also often attempted to convey a specific point of view or an official message. This photograph was taken by a Nazi photographer to celebrate the crushing of the Warsaw ghetto uprising in Poland in 1943. The image was included in leather-bound albums presented as gifts to the head of the SS, Heinrich Himmler, and to two other SS leaders. After the war, the albums were used as evidence in the Nuremberg War Crimes Trials.

The Contradictions of the Subject
Some Nazis would have preferred that this photograph not exist at all. The uprising was an embarrassment, and according to Nazi ideology, Jews should not have had the courage to resist trained, well-armed Nazi troops. The photograph shows that the Jewish revolt has been crushed, but it might also raise questions about whether the Nazis would encounter other armed Jewish uprisings. A German looking at this picture might also ask why it had taken so many German soldiers to capture these three Jews.

The Gender of the Figures
Two of the Jews pictured here are women. It would have been difficult for the soldiers, both those at the uprising and those who saw the photograph later, to understand how such poorly armed women could fight off trained German soldiers for almost three weeks. The fact that the woman on the right has not raised her hands, in apparent defiance of her captor, may also have made any German who saw this image feel uncomfortable.

Introduction

Why should we care about Adolf Hitler, Nazism, and the Holocaust? The fascination of the Nazi period is obvious. Even from the vantage point of the twenty-first century, the Nazi regime is still one of the most dramatic and destructive episodes in western European, indeed in world, history. Nazism is synonymous with terror, concentration camps, and mass murder. Hitler's war claimed tens of millions of lives and left Europe in complete ruins. Nazism has given us words and symbols that continue to strike fear in the hearts of people who otherwise know very little about Hitler or the Nazi regime. Think of the term for Hitler's secret police, "Gestapo," or the ultimate Nazi symbol, the swastika, which has become a twentieth-century shorthand for evil. In 1916, swastikas were prominently displayed on the uniforms of a Canadian girls' hockey team. At that time, well before Hitler's name had become a household word, this symbol could still be seen as a relatively innocent sun wheel. After Hitler, however, it could only mean death, destruction, and racial hatred.

Nazism is therefore important to all of us because of the ways in which it continues to live on in our imaginations. When we reach for a historical comparison to condemn a present-day dictator, Hitler's name comes to mind; politicians and reporters frequently compared Saddam Hussein, the former dictator of Iraq, to Hitler. When we look at pictures on television of genocide in Rwanda, images of the Holocaust may also play before our mind's eye. Since the end of the Second World War, the ghost of Nazism has helped Americans to define who they are. Because the United States played an important role in the coalition that defeated Nazi Germany, Americans can identify themselves as the very opposite of this ultimate evil, embodying all the best traits of democracy that Nazism had tried to destroy.

What was Nazism? The answer to this question has two parts because from 1919 to 1933 Nazism was a political movement and from 1933 to 1945 it was a political regime or state. In the years between the two world wars, from 1918 to 1939, there were several fascist political movements that looked like Nazism. Fascist political

A Nazi leader in Hamburg, Germany, stands in front of a huge swastika in 1933. He tells the assembled citizens they must contribute to the Nazi charity Winter Help.

ideas are extremely conservative, highly nationalistic, and antide-mocratic. Fascists favor a strong central government ruled by a single fascist party that does not allow free speech or the other basic liberties and human rights important to democratic soci-eties. Very few fascist parties have gained enough power to become governments or regimes. Italy was the only other major European country in which a fascist political party came to power under its own steam.

It is hard to imagine fascist movements without World War I. Fascist political parties and ideologies burst on to the political scenes of many European countries after the end of the war in 1918. Europeans turned to these conservative, rigid parties in response to the massive social disorder caused by this war that killed millions of soldiers in the trenches, threatened millions of civilians with starvation, and destroyed several European govern-ments, including those of Russia, Germany, Austria-Hungary, and Italy. German Nazism and other forms of fascism were also intense reactions to the Russian Revolution of 1917 and to the creation of the Soviet Union, a communist dictatorship that threatened to spread its doctrines and influence west across Europe. Communism is an ideology that sees the world divided between two major social classes—capitalists, or owners, and workers—locked in a major struggle with each other that leads to a revolution. In the revolution, the workers seize control of the state and of all indus-try and agriculture, which is then owned and run collectively by the new "workers' state." Fascist movements appealed to those Europeans who feared communism and who felt that the existing democracies were simply too weak to deal with this threat.

Like Italian fascism, German Nazism was fueled by an intense popular and ethnic nationalism. Unlike Italian fascism (and many other European forms of fascism), German Nazism embraced an extreme racial anti-Semitism, a hatred of Jews based on the false assumption that Jews are a distinct and dangerous race or ethnic group. Although some of the characteristics that describe Nazism are true of the entire history of this movement, after 1933 there were significant breaks and differences. The key difference was that after 1933, when the Nazi Party had control of the state, it revealed its vicious, anti-Semitic and racist core beliefs more and more openly and also embarked on a genocidal plan involving the deliberate murder of an entire people.

It is hard to conceive of Nazism without Hitler. Certainly his massive personal popularity gave the Nazi regime a legitimacy it would not have otherwise had. Certainly his program for a racial state and an aggressive war of conquest set the agenda for Germany in the 1930s and 1940s. But, it took many more Germans than just Hitler to fight a war that claimed more than 60 million lives before it was over, and it took many more Germans than the small, criminal band of Nazi leaders to plan, organize, and implement the murder of millions of Jews and other victims of the Nazis' racial hatred. In understanding Nazism, we can only get so far by analyzing Hitler's biography and psychology. Hitler led the way, but he did not simply brainwash or coerce Germans into performing or supporting unspeakably brutal acts of violence and murder. For the nightmare of Nazi ideology and racial hatred to become a lived reality, tens of thousands of Germans (and also non-German accomplices) had to perform criminal deeds willingly, sometimes even quite eagerly, that in any normal world would have brought them at the very least a long prison sentence. In addition to the active perpetrators, many millions more had to be prepared to stand by and say nothing as other human beings were persecuted and killed.

After 1933, Hitler set out his agenda, and defined in general terms the "problems" that needed to be solved—for example, the so-called Jewish problem. But, the particular "solution" to these problems that gained the upper hand at any point was the outcome of fierce competitions for power, and material advantage, among the other Nazi leaders, their subordinates, and the Nazi agencies they commanded. This competition generated ever more extreme answers to the problems Hitler had defined. Coming up with and then implementing the detailed plans eventually involved thousands, probably tens of thousands, of Germans, many of them technical experts and professionals in a variety of fields. These people were not just "following orders," they eagerly developed and implemented new and more efficient ways of, for example, murdering millions of Jews or administering mass sterilization to the "socially undesirable." By no means were all these participants in Hitler's racial program motivated solely by anti-Semitism or racial hatred—the chance to make a career in Nazi Germany could be just as compelling.

Hitler lays the foundation stone for the new Volkswagen factory at Wolfsburg, Germany, in 1938. A storm trooper proudly guards the prototype of the new "People's Car," the design for which eventually became known as the Beetle.

A model of the enormous domed hall that was to be the centerpiece of Hitler's plan to transform Berlin into Germania, the new capital of his vast empire. Had the gigantic structure ever been constructed, it would have been the largest building in the world.

Take the example of Albert Speer, who enjoyed a meteoric rise to power and prominence as Hitler's favorite architect. In 1925, Speer began to study architecture in Berlin. In 1931, after hearing Hitler speak, he joined the Nazi Party. When the Nazis came to power, Speer was given the job of redesigning the ministerial residence of Joseph Goebbels, Hitler's chief of propaganda. The work Speer did on this job brought him to the attention of Hitler, who gave Speer the commission for the new Chancellery building. Together Hitler and Speer then began work on monumental plans to reconstruct Berlin and make it the capital (now to be called Germania) of the new Nazi Empire, with enormous public buildings that would dwarf all existing structures. The Great Hall was intended to be several times the size of St. Peter's Cathedral in Rome, which was then the largest single building in Europe.

Speer managed to complete part of his plan before the war. Part of Berlin was torn down and to house the Aryan Berliners, the people the Nazis considered to be ethnically pure Germans, who had lived in this neighborhood, Speer forcibly evicted Jews from almost six thousand apartments. As armaments minister during the war, Speer worked slave laborers to death to keep the German war machine going. When Germany was defeated, Speer did not think the victorious Allies would prosecute him for war crimes because he had, after all, been only an architect for Hitler. The Allies disagreed. They put Speer on trial in 1945 and sentenced him to twenty years in prison.

It is the active involvement of a large minority of the German population in the crimes of Nazism, combined with the passive acceptance of the great majority that pose the greatest moral problems when we look back on this period of world history. It has often been tempting—not least for the Germans themselves—to see the crimes of Nazism as the work of a small band of criminals who led Germany astray. It is far more troubling to realize, for example, that the dreaded Gestapo, Hitler's secret political police, could never have done its bloody work without the help of literally tens of thousands of ordinary Germans. Citizens eagerly denounced relatives, friends, and neighbors to the secret police for the slightest reason, often only to gain some small personal advantage at the expense, perhaps, of another person's life. What can we think of the German woman who denounced her husband, a former Communist, to the Gestapo simply to make room for her current boyfriend and who told her son that his father would go away and he would get a much better one. What can we say about the thousands of Germans who did not actively engage in the persecution of the Jews but were nonetheless happy to buy Jewish businesses, furniture, and other household items at rock-bottom prices when Jews were forced to emigrate from Germany in the 1930s?

The German people's widespread involvement in Nazi terror, their contribution to the construction of a regime of terror is one of the most dis-

The Shocking Truth About Cola Drinks

POLICE GAZETTE NOV. 25¢

SPORTS · PEOPLE · TRUE ADVENTURE   AMERICA'S FIRST PICTORIAL—EST. 1845

Eichmann's Last Words Reveal:

HITLER IS ALIVE!

Untold Story of Nazi Hideout

WHAT SCANDAL AND FATE HAVE DONE TO LIZ TAYLOR

SECRET LIFE OF
THE MILLIONAIRE BOOKIE WHO LIVED LIKE A BUM

ADOLF HITLER

Told at Last . . . The Real Story . . .
THE BOXING GAME AND MOBSTER CONTRO

The cover of a 1962 issue of the Police Gazette *tabloid announces that Hitler is still alive. Sensational and, of course, untrue stories in popular tabloid newspapers prove the public's continued fascination with Hitler and Nazism.*

turbing features of the twelve years between 1933 and 1945. The Nazi leaders put on trial in Nuremberg, Germany, by the victorious Allies in 1945 were clearly only the tip of a much larger iceberg of participation and complicity in Nazi crimes. But how can we determine which Germans were tainted by their participation in the Nazi regime and which were innocent of all involvement? This has been the key question ever since 1945. It is a moral, not just a legal, question. And, it is a question that has never been easy to answer when we know that even those Germans who just did their jobs properly (such as building tanks and planes) made it possible for the Nazis to continue their war of annihilation until the bitter end.

We can learn about Nazi Germany from an enormous number of sources from the period. These original records include Nazi Party and government documents, many of which were captured by the invading Allied armies when they occupied Germany and are now on deposit in archives in Washington, D.C., and Moscow. We also have the eyewitness reports and memoirs of the people who lived during this time. There is testimony given to the postwar courts established to investigate Nazi war crimes. Many Holocaust survivors have published accounts of their experiences in Nazi concentration camps. There is also a huge array of visual evidence including documentary films and newsreels, photographs, propaganda posters, Nazi art, and images of Nazi architecture.

Chapter One

What Made Nazism Possible?

War, Revolution, and the Weimar Republic

N azi Germany was not inevitable. It took Germany's defeat in World War I and the failure of Germany's first democracy to make Hitler's dictatorship possible. Prior to 1871, there was no nation called Germany, rather there was a collection of small states. The recently formed German Empire entered the First World War severely divided by political, religious, and regional conflicts. Fighting bitter battles from a system of trenches against Britain, France, and Russia for more than four years gave Germans a new sense of national unity. Because of the war, Germans felt they had become members of a national community locked in a life and death struggle against Germany's enemies.

Victory would have made Germany a superpower. But, the Germans were defeated. After living through a bloody war and facing the threat of starvation at home, Germans rose up against their monarchy and, in 1919, replaced it with the Weimar (pronounced "Viemar") Republic, Germany's first democracy. This new democracy started out its short life with several strikes against it. To begin with, there was the lost war. Thirteen million German men had been mobilized to serve in the German Army in World War I. Of these, 1.6 million were killed and 4 million were wounded. By 1918, the British naval blockade had brought Germany to the verge of starvation. If Germany had won the war, Germans would have been rewarded for their suffering and sacrifice by new territories and reparation payments from the defeated British and French. Instead, the Versailles Treaty, the agreement to end the war imposed by the victorious Allies and universally hated by

Packed into a train on their way to the western front, German soldiers display their enthusiasm for the war and their optimism about a quick victory. On the side of the boxcar, they have written "An Excursion to Paris" and "Good-bye to the boulevard [Berlin]."

Germans, stripped Germany of large areas of its territory. The treaty also made Germany demobilize its armed forces. Germany was now to be allowed only an army of 100,000 men, no air force, no submarines, and no weapons of mass destruction, such as poison gas. Germany was also required to pay enormous reparations (compensation for war damage, paid by a defeated enemy).

Many Germans also feared that the revolution that produced the Weimar Republic had opened the door to communism. Inspired by the Russian Revolution of 1917, the small but vocal German Communist Party wanted to ignite a second revolution that would make Germany more like the Soviet Union. Almost all the other political parties insisted that communism was a dangerous threat and anticommunism quickly became a powerful force in Weimar politics, but many thought the Weimar Republic was too weak to stop the communist challenge.

Weimar's dazzling cultural modernity was a third major weakness of the new democracy. This modernity involved cutting-edge experimentation with new styles and forms, in many areas of cultural activity ranging from painting and music to photography and architecture. Germans did not agree about the meaning and

MILITARY OPERATIONS DURING WORLD WAR I

→ Central Powers' offensives (Germany and Austria-Hungary, the Ottoman Empire, and Bulgaria)

◄ Allied Powers' offensives (Britain, France, Russia, Italy, and the U.S.)

— Extent of German advances

⋯⋯ Russan advances

— ·— · Stabilized Western front, December 1914

— — · German advances

— · · — Western front at the armistice, November 1918

the value of modern art, architecture, literature, music or film. For every Weimar German who loved jazz, for example, there were just as many who saw it as an unwelcome import from America that threatened the morals of German young people. The increasing popularity of film, especially movies imported from Hollywood, was likewise seen as a dangerous symptom of the decline of German culture. Modern architects and designers proposed radically new styles. Houses were to become simple "machines for living" with no unnecessary decoration. Yet, to many Germans this type of architecture seemed cold, heartless, and, worst of all, "un-German." In their minds, the flat roofs typical of modern houses belonged in the sunny climate of North Africa. In Germany, only the pointed roof, or what the Nazis later called the German roof, was acceptable.

As if all these problems were not enough, the Weimar Republic also had to deal with the effects of two massive economic crises. Up until 1924, hyperinflation (an extreme devaluation of a nation's currency produced by a massive state budget deficit) ravaged Germany, as no European country had experienced before. During the Great Inflation, as the period from 1918 to 1923 is known, Germans lost faith in their currency, and they began to abandon hope for the future. People who had worked hard and saved money for their retirement found that what they had in the bank was now worthless. Unlike the depression, which began in 1929, the inflation of the early 1920s did not destroy the Weimar Republic. The main reason was that the Weimar government was able to reach an agreement with Germany's former enemies, who reduced the amount of reparations to be paid. The Weimar government was now able to replace the old inflated German currency with a new one that Germans could again trust.

On the other hand, during the worldwide Great Depression, which hit Germany in 1929, no Weimar leader was able to solve the central economic problem, mass unemployment. By 1932, almost 30 percent of the entire population was officially out of work. For many of those who lost their jobs, unemployment was long-term, a matter not of weeks or months but of years. Economic despair translated into votes for the political extremes—the Communists, to whom many of the unemployed now turned, and the Nazis who benefited above all from the growing fear and anxiety among the lower middle classes that Germany was on the edge of the abyss. The increasingly extreme and revolutionary language of the Communist movement served to convince many Germans that there were now only two choices: Hitler or a communist dictator.

Bauhaus architects designed this flat-roofed house in Dessau, Germany, in the 1920s. Critics called this style "un-German" because it looked as if it had come from the sunny south of Europe or even North Africa, and not from northern Europe, where a pointed roof was more appropriate for a rainy and snowy climate.

Memories of a Brutal War

The German war veteran and author Erich Maria Remarque's novel *All Quiet on the Western Front*, published in 1929, presented an uncensored description of the brutality of trench warfare. Machine guns made trench warfare deadly. Attacking forces took heavy casualties before they reached their opponents in the trenches.

We see men living with their skulls blown open; we see soldiers run with their two feet cut off, they stagger on their splintered stumps into the next shell-hole; a lance-corporal crawls a mile and a half on his hands dragging his smashed knee after him; another goes to the dressing station and over his clasped hands bulge his intestines; we see men without mouths, without jaws, without faces; we find one man who has held the artery of his arm in his teeth for two hours in order not to bleed to death. The sun goes down, night comes, the shells whine, life is at an end.

Ernst Jünger, another German writer of the 1920s, had also fought in the trenches. Unlike Remarque, Jünger embraced the war in his 1922 essay, arguing that it had produced a new elite "soldier of steel" who had hardened himself against the psychological effects of massive violence and death.

Two German soldiers lie dead in a trench on the Western Front in 1916. The murderous fire power of machine guns forced soldiers on both sides of the war to seek refuge in trenches dug into the soil of northern and eastern France.

A human is incapable of anything greater than mastering oneself in death. Even the immortal gods must envy him that. We are well armed for our journey, loaded with weapons, explosives, and lighting and signaling instruments, a proper, fighting, shock troop, up to the supreme challenges of modern warfare... They are men forged of steel... They are the best of the modern battlefield, suffused with the reckless spirit of the warrior, whose iron will discharges in clenched, well-aimed bursts of energy... this is the new man, the storm pioneer, the elite of Central Europe. A whole new race, smart, strong, and filled with will... The glowing twilight of a declining age is at once a dawn in which one arms oneself for new, for harder battles... This war is not the end but the prelude to violence.... The war is a great school, and the new man will bear our stamp.... If the advance troops fail to penetrate, if just *one* machine gun remains intact on the other side, these splendid men will be cut down like a herd of deer. That is war. The best and most worthy, the highest embodiment of life, is just good enough to be cast into its insatiable maw. One machine gun, just a second's gliding of the cartridge belt, and these twenty-five men—one could cultivate a sizeable island with them—will hang in tattered bundles from the wire, left slowly to decompose. They are students, cadets with proud old names, mechanics, heirs to fertile estates, saucy big city sorts, and high school students... In the neighboring regiment on the left there bursts a storm of fire. It is a feinting maneuver, to confuse and split enemy artillery. It is just about time. Now the task is to gather oneself. Yes, it is perhaps a pity. Perhaps as well we are sacrificing ourselves for something inessential. But no one can rob us of our value. Essential is not *what* we are fighting for, but *how* we fight. Onward toward the goal, until we triumph or are left behind. The warriors' spirit, the exposure of oneself to risk, even for the tiniest idea, weighs more heavily in the scale than all the brooding about good and evil... We want to show what we have in us; then, if we fall, we will truly have lived to the full.

On the home front, women struggled to find food for their families. The British naval embargo prevented ships from reaching German harbors, depriving Germans of important foodstuffs. Between 1914 and 1918, more than 750,000 Germans died of malnutrition and the diseases it produced. In the so-called 1916–1917 Turnip Winter millions had to survive on an estimated seven to nine hundred calories per day, calories that often came primarily from turnips. As early as 1916, the anger of women who were waiting in the long lines to buy scarce food boiled over into food riots. In May 1916, a Berlin newspaper reported that women had to start waiting in line for food hours before the markets opened.

Whoever, on these chilly spring nights does not shy away from a walk through the streets of the city, will, already before midnight, see figures, loaded down with household utensils, stealing back and forth in front of the covered markets. At first, there are only a few, but with the approach of midnight, the groups become real crowds. These are predominantly composed of women. In the

Berliners cut meat from a dead horse in 1918. By the end of World War I, so many Germans faced starvation that they saw even rotting horse meat as a welcome addition to their meager diet.

palliasse

Thin mattress filled with straw

beginning, they crouch down on the steps of the surrounding shops and on the iron park fences. Soon, however, one [woman] comes and lays a palliasse down near the entrance, on which she makes herself comfortable. That is the signal for general movement. Behind the happy owner of the palliasse, a second woman sets up a deck chair. Close to her, another, less demanding [woman] sits down on a simple wicker chair she transported from her apartment, which is God only knows how far away. A fourth only has a "stick"... The others stand there apathetically, some are sleeping as they stand, and the moonlight makes their pale faces appear even paler. Policemen appear and walk morosely up and down. Morning dawns. New throngs draw near. Women with strollers... Now the coffeepots and sandwiches are going to be brought out. Some of the women reach for their knitting in order to shorten the leaden hours. Finally, the selling begins. And the result: a paltry half a pound or, when one is especially lucky, a whole pound of meat, lard or butter for half of the shoppers, whereas the others have to go away empty-handed.

The Promise and Problems of Weimar Democracy

Although it was the product of defeat and revolution, the Weimar Republic might have eventually been able to win the loyalty of the great majority of Germans. This, after all, was the most democratic system of government Germany had

ever known. The new constitution also promised social rights to its citizens. These became the foundation for a social welfare system that attempted to meet the needs of the hundreds of thousands of German men and women whose lives were damaged by the war, inflation, and, eventually, the Great Depression that started in 1929.

CHAPTER II: FUNDAMENTAL RIGHTS AND DUTIES OF THE GERMANS

Section 1: The Individual

Article 109. All Germans are equal before the law. Men and women have the same fundamental civil rights and duties. Public legal privileges or disadvantages of birth or of rank are abolished. Titles of nobility...may be bestowed no longer.... Orders and decorations shall not be conferred by the state. No German shall accept titles or orders from a foreign government....

Article 114. Personal liberty is inviolable. Curtailment or deprivation of personal liberty by a public authority is permissible only by authority of law.

Persons who have been deprived of their liberty must be informed at the latest on the following day by whose authority and for what reasons they have been held. They shall receive the opportunity without delay of submitting objections to their deprivation of liberty.

Article 115. The house of every German is his sanctuary and is inviolable. Exceptions are permitted only by authority of law....

Article 117. The secrecy of letters and all postal, telegraph, and telephone communications is inviolable. Exceptions are inadmissible except by national law.

Article 118. Every German has the right, within the limits of the general laws, to express his opinion freely by word, in writing, in print, in picture form, or in any other way...Censorship is forbidden...

Section 2: The General Welfare

Article 123. All Germans have the right to assemble peacefully and unarmed without giving notice and without special permission...

Article 124. All Germans have the right to form associations and societies for purposes not contrary to the criminal law...

Article 126. Every German has the right to petition...

Young women workers pose outside the huge Krupp armament factory during World War I. So many German men were drafted to fight in the trenches during the war that women had to take their places in factories and mines to keep war production going.

Section 3: Religion and Religious Societies
Article 135. All inhabitants... enjoy full religious freedom and freedom of conscience. The free exercise of religion is guaranteed by the Constitution and is under public protection...
Article 137. There is no state church...

Section 4: Education and the Schools
Article 142. Art, science, and the teaching thereof are free...
Article 143. The education of the young is to be provided for by means of public institutions....
Article 144. The entire school system is under the supervision of the state...
Article 145. Attendance at school is compulsory...

Section 5: Economic Life
Article 151. The regulation of economic life must be compatible with the principles of justice, with the aim of attaining humane conditions of existence for all. Within these limits the economic liberty of the individual is assured...
Article 159. Freedom of association for the preservation and promotion of labor and economic conditions is guaranteed to everyone and to all vocations. All agreements and measures attempting to restrict or restrain this freedom [are] unlawful...
Article 161. The Reich shall organize a comprehensive system of [social] insurance...
Article 165. Workers and employees are called upon to cooperate, on an equal footing, with employers in the regulation of wages and of the conditions of labor, as well as in the general development of the productive forces...

The chances that Weimar democracy would succeed were severely limited by the Versailles Treaty. One of the key provisions of the treaty was Article 231, the so-called War Guilt Clause, which made Germany accept complete responsibility for starting World War I. The victorious Allies felt that this admission of guilt justified all the other requirements of the Versailles Treaty, such as the demand for financial reparations in Article 232.

Article 231. The Allied and Associated Governments affirm and Germany accepts the responsibility of Germany and her allies for causing all the loss and damage to which the Allied and Associated Governments and their nationals have been subjected

A 1930 election poster for the left-wing Social Democratic Party depicts the types of people forced into poverty by World War I and the postwar inflation: a soldier blinded in the trenches, a young mother who lost her husband in the war, an old man without a pension, and two children who lost their father in the war. The caption reads: "Don't abandon us! Defend social welfare! Vote List 1 Social Democrats."

as a consequence of the war imposed upon them by the aggression of Germany and her allies.

Article 232. . . . The Allied and Associated Governments. . . require, and Germany undertakes, that she will make compensation for all damage done to the civilian population of the Allied and Associated Powers and to their property during the period of the belligerency of each as an Allied or Associated Power against Germany by such aggression by land, by sea and from the air, and in general all damage as defined in Annex I hereto.

The young Weimar democracy had to defend itself against widely circulated claims that the German Army had not actually lost the war at the front. According to this myth, the defeat was really the fault of left-wing agitators who cut the ground out from under the German Army by starting the revolution that led to the founding of the republic. This "stab-in-the-back" legend branded as traitors the members of all left-wing political parties, including the Social Democratic Party, the largest and most moderate of the left-wing groups, which helped to govern the Weimar Republic in its early days. Figures in the army, such as field marshall Paul von Hindenburg, helped to sell the "stab-in-the-back" legend to the German public because it diverted attention from their own military failures. In 1919, von Hindenburg presented this myth to a parliamentary committee, which made a public record of his testimony.

The concern as to whether the homeland would remain resolute until the war was won. . . never left us. We often raised a warning voice to the Reich government. . . . The obedient troops who remained immune to revolutionary attrition suffered greatly from the behavior, in violation of duty, of their revolutionary comrades; they had to carry the battle the whole time.

(Chairman's bell. Commotion and shouting.)

Chairman: Please continue, General Field Marshal.

von Hindenburg: The intentions of the command could no longer be executed. Our repeated proposals for strict discipline and strict legislation were not adopted. Thus did our operations necessarily miscarry; the *collapse* was inevitable; the revolution only provided the keystone.

An English general said with justice: "The German army was stabbed in the back." No guilt applies to the good core of the army. Its achievements are just as admirable as those of the officer

During the German revolution at the end of World War I, representatives of the left-liberal Democratic Party march in a demonstration against the extreme left-wing Spartacist movement. Such parties as the German Democratic Party and the Social Democrats were more concerned about the threat of a Russian-style seizure of power by the Spartacists than about the danger of a counter revolution led by right-wing forces.

corps. Where the guilt lies has clearly been demonstrated. If it needed more proof, then it would be found in the quoted statement of the English general and in the boundless astonishment of our enemies at their victory.

That is the general trajectory of the tragic development of the war for Germany, after a series of brilliant, unsurpassed successes on many fronts, following an accomplishment by the army and the people for which no praise is high enough.

To many Germans, the German Revolution and the Weimar Republic appeared to have made their country vulnerable to communism. Impressed by the example of the 1917 Russian Revolution, extreme left-wing political radicals insisted that German workers must now make a similar communist revolution in Germany. In Russia, a small group of revolutionaries called Bolsheviks led by Vladimir Ilyich Lenin seized power in Moscow and St. Petersburg. The revolutionaries overthrew the provisional government that replaced the Czar (the royal ruler of the Russian Empire), who had been dethroned because the war was going so badly for Russia. In November

1918, the German Spartacist League—the predecessor to the German Communist Party that was named for an uprising of slaves in ancient Rome—issued a manifesto to German workers and their colleagues around the world.

PROLETARIANS! MEN AND WOMEN OF LABOR! COMRADES!

The revolution has made its entry into Germany. The masses of the soldiers, who for four years were driven to the slaughterhouse for the sake of capitalistic profits, and the masses of workers, who for four years were exploited, crushed, and starved, have revolted. That fearful tool of oppression—Prussian [the German state that was the core of the German nation formed in 1871] militarism, that scourge of humanity—lies broken on the ground. Its most noticeable representatives, and therewith the most noticeable of those guilty of this war, the Kaiser [emperor] and the Crown Prince, have fled from the country. Workers' and soldiers' councils have been formed everywhere. . . . the hour has struck for a settlement with capitalist class rule . . . The imperialism of all countries knows no "understanding"; it knows only one right—capital's profits; it knows only one language—the sword; it knows only one method—violence. And if it is now talking in all countries, in yours as well as ours, about the "League of Nations," "disarmament," "rights of small nations," "self-determination of the peoples," it is merely using the customary lying phrases of the rulers for the purpose of lulling to sleep the watchfulness of the proletariat.

Proletarians of all countries! This must be the last war! We owe that to the twelve million murdered victims; we owe that to our children; we owe that to humanity.

Europe has been ruined through the infamous international murder. Twelve million bodies cover the gruesome scenes of the imperialistic crime. The flower of youth and the best men of the nations have been mowed down. Uncounted productive forces have been annihilated. Humanity is almost ready to bleed to death from the bloodletting. Victors and vanquished stand at the

proletarian

Term used mainly by socialists and communists to describe men and women who performed manual labor, usually in a factory, for an hourly wage

A figure representing German communism slays the many-headed monster of militarism, capitalism, and the landed aristocracy. In this poster, the left-wing Spartacus group, which later became the German Communist Party, is the defender of the German working class against its reactionary enemies.

edge of the abyss... Socialism alone is in a position to complete the great work of permanent peace, to heal the thousand wounds from which humanity is bleeding, to transform the plains of Europe, trampled down by the apocryphal horsemen of war, into blossoming gardens, to conjure up ten productive forces for every one destroyed, to awaken all the physical and moral energies of humanity, and to replace hatred and dissension with fraternal solidarity, harmony, and respect for every human being....

Proletarians of all countries... we now summon you to a common struggle... If your ruling classes succeed in throttling the proletarian revolution in Germany, as well as in Russia, then they will turn against you with redoubled violence. Your capitalists hope that victory over us and over revolutionary Russia will give them the power to scourge you with a whip of scorpions and to erect the thousand-year empire of exploitation upon the grave of socialism.

Therefore the proletariat of Germany is looking toward you in this hour. Germany is pregnant with the social revolution, but socialism can be realized only by the proletariat of the world.

And therefore we call to you: "Arise for the struggle! Arise for action! The time for empty manifestoes... and high-sounding words has passed!..." We ask you to elect workers' and soldiers' councils everywhere that will seize political power and, together with us, will restore peace... Peace is to be concluded under the waving banner of the socialist world revolution.

Workers and Soldiers Unite

Local committees of workers and soldiers formed during the revolution took over many tasks normally performed by the regular government. Some radicals saw these bodies as revolutionary forms of direct democracy. They bore certain similarities to the Soviets or revolutionary councils formed during the Russian Revolution.

A skeletal figure of death, representing Russian communism, leaves behind the villages it burned and people it murdered as it moves west toward Germany. This poster encouraged Germans to support the associations formed to fight the spread of communism. The caption reads: Join the Anti-Bolshevist League.

Tretet der Antibolschewistischen Liga bei
Berlin W. Lützowstr: 107.

The New Woman and the Movies

Weimar's modern culture was exciting and attractive to many Germans. Other Germans thought postwar cultural developments were dangerously immoral. Relations between men and women were an important arena for the culture wars that erupted between divided Germans. At least some of the younger generation of German women were no longer prepared to accept a traditionally subordinate role. This spirit of rebellion is reflected in a popular cabaret song, "Chuck Out the Men," written by Friedrich Hollaender in 1926.

The battle for emancipation
's been raging since hist'ry began
Yes, feminists of every nation
want to throw off the chains made by man
. . .
hear all our voices thunder in protest
Anything that men do women can do too
and more than that we women do it best
Chuck all the men out of the Reichstag
and chuck all the men out of the courthouse
Men are the problem with humanity
they're blinded by their vanity
Women have passively embraced them
when we could have easily outpaced them
Yes we should have long ago replaced them
or better yet erased them
If we haven't made our feelings clear we women have had it up
to here
. . .
The men get their pick of the professions
they're policemen or scholars or clerks
They get rich and acquire possessions
like we wives who keep houses for these jerks
They're ruining the country while we mop the floor
They're flushing this whole nation down
the drain
Sisters stand together, let's show
these men the door before they drive us totally insane
Chuck all the men out, etc.

Reichstag
Parliament

The German film actress Marlene Dietrich takes the image of the "New Woman" to extremes by dressing in a man's tuxedo and top hat. There is an element of parody in the way Dietrich presents herself, but conservative Germans did not like the joke. Dietrich left Berlin for Hollywood before Hitler came to power.

The New Woman was one of the most visible symbols of Weimar's modern culture. Like her American counterpart, the flapper, the German New Woman displayed her emancipation from traditional gender roles by wearing short hair and trousers. She might smoke and she certainly acted in public as if she had all the same rights as men. Conservatives saw the New Woman as a dangerous threat to the family. In 1929, Elsa Herrmann, an advocate of women's rights, published a book, *This Is the New Woman*, that offered a less threatening image of the New Woman but which nonetheless demanded new roles for women and insisted upon equality between men and women.

The woman of yesterday lived exclusively for and geared her actions toward the future. Already as a half-grown child, she toiled and stocked her hope chest for her future dowry.

In the first years of marriage she did as much of the household work as possible herself to save on expenses, thereby laying the foundation for future prosperity, or at least worry-free old age… The woman of yesterday pursued the same goal of securing the future in all social spheres, varied only according to her specific conditions… Her primary task, however, she naturally saw to be caring for the well-being of her children, the ultimate carriers of her thoughts on the future. Thus the purpose of her existence was in principle fulfilled once the existence of these children had been secured, that is, when she had settled the son in his work and gotten the daughter married. Then she collapsed completely, like a good racehorse collapses when it has maintained its exertions up to the very last minute…

In stark contrast, the woman of today is oriented exclusively toward the present… For the sake of her economic independence, the necessary precondition for the development of a self-reliant personality, she seeks to support herself through gainful employment. It is only too obvious that, in contrast to earlier times, this conception of life necessarily involves a fundamental change in the orientation of women toward men which acquires its basic tone from concerns of equality and comradeship.

The new woman has set herself the goal of proving in her work and deeds that the representatives of the female sex are not second-class persons existing only in dependence and obedience but are fully capable of satisfying the demands of their positions in life. The proof of her personal value and the proof of the value of her sex are therefore the maxims ruling the life of every single woman of our times, for the sake of herself and the sake of the whole. . . .

The people of yesterday are strongly inclined to characterize the modern woman as unfeminine because she is no longer wrapped up in kitchen work and the chores that have to be done around the house . . .

Despite the fact that every war from time immemorial has entailed the liberation of an intellectually, spiritually, or physically fettered social group, the war and postwar period of our recent past has brought women nothing extraordinary in the slightest but only awakened them from their lethargy and laid upon them the responsibility for their own fate. Moreover, the activity of women in our recent time of need represented something new neither to themselves nor to the population as a whole, since people had long been theorizing the independence and equality of woman in her relationship to man.

The new woman is therefore no artificially conjured phenomenon, consciously conceived in opposition to an existing system; rather, she is organically bound up with economic and cultural developments of the last few decades. Her task is to clear the way for equal rights for women in all areas of life. That does not mean that she stands for complete equality of the representatives of both sexes. Her goal is much more to achieve recognition for the complete legitimacy of women as human beings, according to each the right to have her particular physical constitution and her accomplishments respected and, where necessary, protected.

The New Woman of Weimar Germany could often be found at the movies. German conservatives complained that each week in thousands of movie houses all across Germany, far too many Germans sought escape from reality in the movie dream worlds manufactured by Hollywood or its German equivalent, the massive UFA studios. Siegfried Kracauer was an astute observer of Weimar culture. Although he was certainly no conservative, he harshly criticized the fantasies nourished by the movies of the time. In his 1927 essay, "The Little Shopgirls Go to the Movies," Kracauer argued that even a light-hearted romance film encouraged young women to accept a distorted view of the way society actually operated.

In reality it may not often happen that a scullery maid marries the owner of a Rolls Royce. But doesn't every Rolls Royce owner dream that scullery maids dream of rising to his stature? Stupid

A poster advertises the 1927 movie Metropolis, *a science-fiction film set in a futuristic urban society. Film was one of the most popular new forms of mass entertainment, and millions of Germans escaped to the movies every week.*

What has been achieved in this German film leaves all the American accomplishments in cinematography in the dust, and is unique in the history of cinema.

—Screenwriter Willy Haas writing in a 1927 film magazine about the movie *Metropolis*

and unreal film fantasies are the *daydreams of society,* in which its... otherwise repressed wishes take on form...In the endless sequence of films, a limited number of typical themes recur again and again; they reveal how society wants to see itself...The series "The Little Shopgirls Go to the Movies" is conceived as a small collection of samples...

Kracauer then analyzes one recent romance film.

The Golden Heart

A young Berlin wholesaler, an industrious manager of a first-rate company, visits a business friend of his father's in Vienna; the paternal friend's firm is going to pieces because of the disorder in Austria. The guest would leave, if it were not for the business friend's daughter, a sweet Viennese gal who makes it clear to him that there are other things besides management: the waves of the Danube and the wine gardens specializing in new vintages. With delight, the young man from Berlin discovers his dormant feelings. He cleans up the company, which will soon be turning a profit again, and gets the gal...Even without close-ups, this course of events would be believable. Whether in the city of waltz dreams or on the beautiful beaches of the Neckar—someplace, but not here in the present, the rich are falling in love and discovering in the process that they have hearts. It is not true that they are heartless: films refute what life would make one believe...The little shopgirls learn to understand that their brilliant boss is made of gold on the inside as well; they await the day when they can revive a young Berliner with their silly little hearts.

In 1930, the German Textile Workers Trade Union asked women textile workers to describe their normal working day. These working women would certainly not have been able to see their own lives reflected in the image of the New Woman, who was economically independent, sexually liberated, and an avid consumer of film and other forms of modern mass culture. A Bavarian textile worker who responded to the survey described her daily tasks.

As far as I'm concerned, the work at home would be enough.... The workday begins at 4:45. Make the beds, comb my hair, feed Mizzi and the rabbits, drink something warm, and the clock reads 5:30. It is time to go to the factory. Lunch box and coffee thermos in hand, and it's off to the work bench. 6:00 start, year in, year out. I do my work standing. We work nine and a half hours a day. 8:30 to 9:00 in the morning we have a break to eat. In this half hour I usually have a lot of socks with me to darn, because the time at home is short. Back to work at 9:00 until 12:00. From 12:00 to 1:00 in the afternoon is lunchtime. I usually have some mending to do; sometimes a letter to write as well. At 1:00 it starts up again until 5:00 or 5:30—after twelve hours away, back home!

Without a rest it's off to the stove to prepare lunch for the coming day. Then washing, drying, a bit of dinner, finishing by 9:00 in the evening at the latest. Then I'm finished too and want nothing but some peace.

Thursday evenings the wash is usually put in to soak. Friday evening it's washed, Saturday morning hung out to dry. Afterwards it's off to the factory till 12:00. Sunday morning is for ironing, often for baking too, but always for cooking for Sunday and Monday. Sunday afternoon (usually in the winter) I mend the linen and clean up. At 4:00 I can rest a little.

My view is that if a housewife and mother could be at home, then the household and children would be better served. In France,

By 1923, it made more sense to use German banknotes as fuel or as wallpaper, as this man does, than to try to buy anything with the worthless paper currency.

Alsace, and Saxony the women do not work in the factory and their life is easier than in Bavaria. In Bavaria the poor women live like slaves, so to speak. (Housewife, mother, factory worker.)

Economic Crises

Moritz Julius Bonn was a German economist who frequently served as an expert adviser for the German government and international commissions in the 1920s. In his 1948 autobiography, *Wandering Scholar*, he described his personal experience of the final phase of the Great Inflation in Germany during the summer of 1923.

One morning I arrived in Munich on my way to the country. While strolling outside the station, I ran into an acquaintance, a charming woman, who almost embraced me in public. "Do give me something to eat," she said, "I am famished. I went to the country," she explained, "with a supply of five-dollar bills. Yesterday the mark broke so rapidly that nobody could change one for me. I had no dinner; I took the earliest train to town this morning; I am waiting for the banks to open, and hope that they have enough marks to change a five-dollar note. I would have had to go without breakfast, if I had not met you." During the late phases of the inflation such experiences were common. Anybody who had foreign exchange was rich, provided that his money was in sufficiently small denominations to make an exchange possible...

We had rented a farmhouse in Bavaria, where my wife lived most of the year, and where I used to spend my vacations. We kept one or two cows and had a vegetable garden; fields and pastures were leased. Our neighbors were farmers, owning isolated holdings on the top of hills similar to ours. They depended mainly on dairy farming and the sale of young livestock... These farmers did not suffer badly... they would not sell anything against marks , though they did a lively trade by way of barter. For a pair of old flannel trousers or a few leather straps we could buy grain to feed our cows... They were more than eager to sell goods against foreign currency, the acceptance of which was forbidden—but nobody cared any longer for the law.... Goods were becoming much more valuable than money.

... Artisans and tradespeople in our village were very much worse off than farmers, since they could not get sufficient food from their small plots of land. Raw materials were scarce, and they had few opportunities for making goods...

Workers were not the chief sufferers. Thanks to strong trade unions, their wages were regularly revised upward, though generally with a lag. In the earlier stages…unemployment was low, as it always is during the inflation upswing. For this reason labor had not strongly insisted upon stabilization. Accounting was becoming a nightmare. Before the war a weekly wage of ten dollars was written in two numerals; it now took seven or nine. An army of clerks had to be recruited, and as many of them were inexperienced, business became very involved—prices were being quoted in millions…Banking activities were feverish. Most banks added new floors to their buildings to house new employees. Yet they were no longer keen on getting customers. The handling of an account of 100,000 marks was expensive when its gold value had shrunk to 25 dollars, so they asked depositors, frequently in rather peremptory language, to take away their accounts. Wages were adjusted at least twice a week according to dollar quotations; so were salaries of civil servants. Most of them asked for cash and rushed immediately to the shops to buy such goods as were available. A few hours later the mark might have gone down 100 per cent, and the purchasing power of their salaries might have been halved. . . .

When it was all over, the social structure of Germany had been profoundly altered. The steady middle class, closely connected, though not identical, with the professions, was proletarianized at a time when the rising working class ceased to consider itself proletarian and was ready for incorporation with the middle class. It was a genuine revolution, far more devastating than the political collapse in the autumn of 1918 had been.

By 1924, the inflation was over. But from 1929 onward, Germany was ravaged by an even worse economic crisis than the Great Inflation, an unprecedented depression that bankrupted thousands of businesses, threw millions out of work and brought the country to the very edge of social chaos. In 1933, German writer Hans Fallada published *Little*

This German banknote, issued during the inflation, was worth half a million marks. In January 1921, one U.S. dollar was worth 64.9 German marks. By November 1923, one dollar could buy 4,200,000,000,000 marks.

proletarianized

Pushed into a social position similar to that of the working class because the inflation robbed these middle-class Germans of their pensions and investments

Man, What Now?, a realistic novel about a sales clerk, Johannes Pinneberg, his wife, Bunny, and their infant child. It chronicles their progressive decline into unemployment and homelessness. Finding himself on the Friedrichstrasse, a major street in the center of Berlin, the once respectable Pinneberg, who has been without a job for some time, realizes he has become a social outcast.

For the fourth time Pinneberg was pacing that section of the Friedrichstrasse that lies between the Leipziger and the Linden. He could not go home, he simply revolted at the thought. When he got home, everything was again at a dead end, life flickered into a dim and hopeless distance. But here something still might happen. It was true that the girls did not look at him; a man with so threadbare a coat, such dirty trousers and without a collar did not exist for the girls on the Friedrichstrasse. If he wanted anything of that kind, he had better go along to the Schlesischer; there they did not mind appearances so long as the man could pay. But did he want a girl?

Perhaps he did, he was not sure, he thought no more of the matter. He just wanted to tell some human being what his life had once been, the smart suits he had had, and talk about—

He had entirely forgotten the boy's butter and bananas, it was now nine o'clock and all the shops would be shut! Pinneberg was furious with himself, and even more sorry than angry; he could not go home empty-handed, what would Bunny think of him? Perhaps he could get something at the side-door of a shop. There was a great grocer's shop, radiantly illuminated. Pinneberg flattened his nose against the window. Perhaps there was still someone about. He must get that butter and bananas!

A voice behind him said in a low tone: "Move on please!"

Pinneberg started—he was really quite frightened. A policeman stood beside him.

Was the man speaking to him?

"Move on there, do you hear?" said the policeman, loudly now.

There were other people standing at the shop-window, well-dressed people, but to them the policeman had undoubtedly not addressed himself. He meant Pinneberg.

"What? But why—? Can't I?—"

He stammered; he simply did not understand.

"Are you going?" asked the policeman. "Or shall I—?"

The loop of his rubber club was slipped round his wrist, and he raised the weapon slightly.

Everyone stared at Pinneberg. Some passers-by had stopped, a little crowd began to collect. The people looked on expectantly, they took no sides in the matter; on the previous day shop-windows had been broken on the Friedrich and the Leipziger.

The policeman had dark eyebrows, bright resolute eyes, a straight nose, red cheeks, and an energetic moustache.

"Well?" said the policeman calmly.

Pinneberg tried to speak; Pinneberg looked at the policeman; his lips quivered, and he looked at the bystanders. A little group was standing round the window, well-dressed people, respectable people, people who earned money.

But in the mirror of the window still stood a lone figure, a pale phantom, collarless, clad in a shabby ulster and tar-smeared trousers.

Suddenly Pinneberg understood everything; in the presence of this policeman, these respectable persons, this gleaming window, he understood that he was outside it all, that he no longer belonged here and that he was rightly chased away; he had slipped into the abyss, and was engulfed. Order and cleanliness; they were of the past. So too were work and safe subsistence. And past too were progress and hope. Poverty was not merely misery, poverty was an offence, poverty was evil, poverty meant that a man was suspect.

"Do you want one on the bean?" asked the policeman. Pinneberg obeyed; he was aware of nothing but a longing to hurry to the Friedrichstrasse station and catch his train and get back to Bunny.

Pinneberg was conscious of a blow on his shoulder, not a heavy blow, but just enough to land him in the gutter.

"Beat it" said the policeman. "And be quick about it!"

Pinneberg went; he shuffled along in the gutter close to the curb and thought of a great many things, of fires and bombs and street shooting and how Bunny and the baby were done for: it was all over. . . but really his mind was vacant.

An unemployed young man stands at a street fair in 1930. His shoes have long since worn out, been pawned, or stolen and he is so poor that he cannot afford new ones.

Chapter Two

Enter Hitler

Who was the man to whom increasing numbers of German voters turned in the early 1930s? Adolf Hitler was born on April 20, 1889, in the small Austrian village of Braunau Am Inn just across the border from Bavaria in southern Germany. Hitler's father, an Austrian customs official, died in 1903. Two years later, at age sixteen, Hitler dropped out of school. When he was eighteen, dreaming of becoming an artist, Hitler went to Vienna and took the entrance exam for the school of painting at the Academy of Fine Arts. He failed. In December 1907, Hitler's mother, Klara, died of breast cancer. In October 1908, he again applied to the Vienna Academy, but this time his drawings were judged to be so poor that he was not even allowed to take the formal exam. Yet, he stayed on in Vienna, living in rented rooms and shelters for the homeless, earning some money by occasional day labor or by painting postcards that he sold to tourists.

During his time in Vienna, Hitler became extremely interested in politics and spent long hours arguing about political ideas with the other men in the homeless shelter. Although he was a citizen of the Austro-Hungarian Empire, Hitler saw himself as an ethnic German who had been excluded by the mistakes of history from the new German Empire to the north. In Vienna, Hitler added racial anti-Semitism and a deep hatred of Marxism to his already intense German nationalism.

In 1913, Hitler moved to Munich in Bavaria to avoid military service in the multiethnic Habsburg Empire, as the Austro-Hungarian Empire was also known, which he had grown to hate. But, when World War I broke out in the summer of 1914, Hitler eagerly volunteered to defend his adopted German fatherland. The war gave new meaning to his life. He served on the Western Front, won the Iron Cross, but never rose above the rank of corporal. In October 1918, he was temporarily blinded by a British chlorine gas attack. Hitler was devastated by the defeat of Germany and by the revolution that overthrew the monarchy

In this 1928 photograph, Hitler wears a military uniform and the Iron Cross he earned as a soldier in World War I.

in November 1918. He refused to believe that the German Army actually lost the war. Instead, he blamed Jews and Marxists for undermining the German war effort. In the summer of 1919, Hitler was still in the army, working as a political agent to combat the spread of Marxist ideas among the returning soldiers.

In September 1919, he was told to investigate a small extremist, anti-Semitic group in Munich known as the German Workers' Party, one of many new völkisch (intensely nationalist and racist) splinter groups that formed at the end of the war. He was supposed to find out whether this small organization's propaganda could be useful in the army's attempts to fight the spread of left-wing ideas among the returning soldiers. Instead, Hitler joined the party. Here he found a calling as a rabble-rousing political speaker. The insignificance of this small political fringe group allowed Hitler to make a political career that would never have been open to him in any of the major existing political parties. In February 1920, Hitler changed the party's name to National Socialist German Worker's Party, sometimes called the Nazi Party [in contraction of the party's full title]. The new name signaled his desire to win German workers away from what he called the poisonous "Jewish Teachings of Marxism" and back to the cause of the German nation. Because Karl Marx was a Jew, Hitler insisted that Marxism was an alien set of ideas that could only have negative consequences for Germans. In his view, Marxism encouraged them to see themselves as a society of classes warring with each other rather than as a race in competition with other races.

In early November 1923, the French and Belgians occupied the industrial Ruhr region in western Germany to force the Germans to pay reparations for World War I. At the same time, the postwar hyperinflation spiraled completely out of control. Hitler thought the time was ripe to overthrow the new democratic republic with force. His attempt to take control of the Munich government in early November 1923 failed because the army authorities refused to support him. Hitler was put on trial but received a light seven-month prison term.

The failure of this attempt to seize power convinced Hitler that the Nazis would have to conquer the Weimar

Hitler (first man on the left) poses with his fellow soldiers in 1916. In his life as a politician, Hitler emphasized that he had once been an ordinary soldier in the trenches, just like millions of other Germans.

Republic by legal, electoral means. Yet, when Hitler emerged from jail at the end of 1924, only 3 percent of the electorate took the Nazis seriously enough to vote for them. Germany was no longer in a state of crisis. The Nazis did not do much better at the polls until September 1930, when they increased their vote to 18.3 percent. By July 1932 they had become the single largest party in the German parliament with 230 seats and 37.4 percent of the popular vote. At least four factors produced this meteoric ascent: the weaknesses of Weimar democracy; the catastrophic Great Depression; the Nazis' ability to exploit the grievances of voters unhappy with the existing political options; and the growing desire of leading figures in industry, agriculture, the army, the government bureaucracy, as well as ordinary voters to replace Weimar democracy with some type of authoritarian rule by a strong leader. Despite his increasing popularity, Hitler never gained an absolute majority in elections. He could never simply demand to be made chancellor (prime minister, head of government in this parliamentary system), but had to be "lifted" into power by the president and other powerful government leaders.

From the War to the Failed Attempt to Seize Power in 1923

Adolf Hitler claimed that Jews could never be assimilated into German society, that Jews would always be dangerously different because their biology (what we might call their genes) made them think, feel, and act differently than Aryan (racially pure) Germans. In September 1919, Hitler wrote his first statement about the "Jewish problem" in response to a letter from one of his fellow participants in a German Army indoctrination course.

If the danger represented by the Jews today finds expression in the undeniable dislike of them felt by a larger section of our people, the cause of this dislike is on the whole not to be found in the clear recognition of the corrupting activity of the Jews generally among our people . . . it originates mainly through personal relationships, from the impression left behind him by the individual Jew and which is almost invariably unfavorable. Antisemitism thereby acquires only too easily the character of being a manifestation of emotion. But this is wrong. Antisemitism as a political movement must not be, cannot be, determined by emotional criteria, but

It makes no difference whether they laugh at us or revile us, whether they represent us as clowns or criminals; the main thing is that they mention us, that they concern themselves with us again and again, and that we gradually in the eyes of the workers themselves appear to be the only power that anyone reckons with at the moment.

—Adolf Hitler,
Mein Kampf, 1925

The only stable emotion is hate.
—Adolf Hitler in a speech
to the Hamburg National
Club, 1926

only through the recognition of facts. The facts are as follows: First, the Jews are definitely a race and not a religious community. The Jew himself never calls himself a Jewish German, a Jewish Pole, a Jewish American, but only a German, a Polish, an American Jew... The feelings of the Jews are concerned with purely material things; his thoughts and desires even more so. The dance round the golden calf becomes a ruthless struggle for all those goods which, according to our innermost feelings, should not be the highest and most desirable things on earth... His activities produce a racial tuberculosis among nations.... antisemitism based on reason must lead to the systematic legal combating and removal of the rights of the Jew, which he alone of foreigners living among us possesses (legislation to make them aliens). Its final aim, however, must be the uncompromising removal of the Jews altogether. Both are possible only under a government of national strength, never under a government of national impotence.

Hitler's insistence that Jews could never be Germans quickly found expression in the Nazi Party program presented by Hitler to a meeting on February 24, 1920.

4. None but members of the nation may be citizens of the state. None but those of German blood, whatever their creed, may be members of the nation. No Jew therefore may be a member of the nation.

Most of the early recruits to the Nazi movement were less interested in the specifics of the party program than in Hitler himself. Hitler's abilities as a fiery speaker soon made him into a local sensation. People started to come to Nazi Party meetings just to hear Hitler. Hitler was convinced that the spoken word was much more powerful than any written statement of a political idea. In his 1925 political manifesto, *Mein Kampf*, meaning "my struggle," he explained why.

While the speaker gets a continuous correction of his speech from the crowd he is addressing, since he can always see in the faces of his listeners to what extent they can follow his arguments with understanding and whether the impression and the effect of his words lead to the desired goal—the writer does not know his readers at all. Therefore, to begin with, he will not aim at a definite mass before his eyes, but will keep his arguments entirely general. By this to a certain degree he loses psychological subtlety and in

Hitler's face glares out from the cover of his book Mein Kampf *(My Struggle), published in 1925. This political manifesto set out the key features of Hitler's ideology: intense nationalism, hatred of the Weimar Republic, the Versailles Treaty, and the Jewish and Marxist conspiracy that had imposed this shame upon the German nation.*

Hitler's main political asset was his ability to captivate his audience as a public speaker. By 1925, he had already become a local political sensation in Munich.

consequence suppleness. And so, by and large, a brilliant speaker will be able to write better than a brilliant writer can speak, unless he continuously practices this art. On top of this there is the fact that the mass of people as such is lazy; that they remain inertly in the spirit of their old habits and, left to themselves, will take up a piece of written matter only reluctantly if it is not in agreement with what they themselves believe and does not bring them what they had hoped for. Therefore, an article with a definite tendency is for the most part read only by people who can already be reckoned to this tendency. . .

To my mind, the speaker can treat the same theme as the book; he will, if he is a brilliant popular orator, not be likely to repeat the same reproach and the same substance twice in the same form. He will always let himself be borne by the great masses in such a way that instinctively the very words come to his lips that he needs to speak to the hearts of his audience. And if he errs, even in the slightest, he has the living correction before him. . . If—firstly— he sees that they do not understand him, he will become so primitive and clear in his explanations that even the last member of his audience has to understand him; if he feels—secondly—that they cannot follow him, he will construct his ideas so cautiously and slowly that even the weakest member of the audience is not left behind, and he will—thirdly—if he suspects that they do not seem convinced of the soundness of his argument, repeat it over and over in constantly new examples. He himself will utter their objections, which he senses though unspoken, and go on confuting them and exploding them, until at length even the last group of an opposition, by its very bearing and facial expression, enables him to recognize its capitulation to his arguments.

Here again it is not seldom a question of overcoming prejudices which are not based on reason, but, for the most part unconsciously, are supported only by sentiment. To overcome this barrier of instinctive aversion, of emotional hatred, of prejudiced rejection, is a thousand times harder than to correct a faulty or erroneous scientific opinion. False concepts and poor knowledge can be eliminated by instruction, the resistance of the emotions never. Here only an appeal to these mysterious powers themselves can be effective; and the writer can hardly ever accomplish this, but almost exclusively the orator.

The listeners who found Hitler so compelling were not simply hypnotized by his verbal fireworks. Germans who were drawn to Hitler were often looking for the kind of emotional experience he had to offer, as Kurt Ludecke, one of Hitler's early associates, admitted in his 1938 memoir. Ludecke first heard Hitler speak in 1922.

My critical faculty was swept away. Leaning from the rostrum as if he were trying to impel his inner self into the consciousness of all these thousands, he was holding the masses, and me with them, under an hypnotic spell by the sheer force of his conviction... He seemed another Luther. I forgot everything but the man; then glancing around, I saw that his magnetism was holding these thousands as one. Of course I was ripe for this experience. I was a man of thirty-two, weary with disgust and disillusionment, a wanderer seeking a cause, a patriot without a channel for his patriotism, a yearner after the heroic without a hero. I experienced an exaltation that could be likened only to religious conversion.

Hitler's failed attempt to seize power in 1923 should have been the end of his political career. Instead, he was able to use his trial to reach a national audience for the first time. Reporters came from all over Germany to hear Hitler's defense. In his concluding statement at his trial, Hitler cleverly presented himself not as an ordinary politician seeking power but as an unselfish crusader.

I aimed from the first at something a thousand times higher than being a minister. I wanted to become the destroyer of Marxism. I am going to achieve this task, and, if I do, the title of minister will be an absurdity as far as I am concerned....

Luther

Martin Luther led the Protestant Reformation and founded Lutheranism in the sixteenth-century

At one time I believed that perhaps this battle against Marxism could be carried on with the help of the government. In January 1923 I learned that that was just not possible. The hypothesis for the victory of Marxism is not that Germany must be free, but rather Germany will only be free when Marxism is broken. At that time I did not dream that our movement would become great and cover Germany like a flood.

The army that we are building grows from day to day, from hour to hour. Right at this moment I have the proud hope that once the hour strikes these wild troops will merge into battalions, battalions into regiments, regiments into divisions. I have hopes that the old cockade will be lifted from the dirt, that the old colors will be unfurled to flutter again, that expiation will come before the tribunal of God. Then from our bones and from our graves will speak the voice of the only tribunal which has the right to sit in justice over us.

Then, gentlemen, not you will be the ones to deliver the verdict over us, but that verdict will be given by the eternal judgment of history, which will speak out against the accusation that has been made against us. I know what your judgment will be. But that other court will not ask us:

Have you committed high treason or not? That court will judge us, the quartermaster-general of the old army, its officers and soldiers, who as Germans wanted only the best for their people and Fatherland, who fought and who were willing to die. You might just as well find us guilty a thousand times, but the goddess

Hitler (fourth from right) poses with other participants in the November 1923 attempt to overthrow the German government. Although the attempt to seize power failed miserably, the treason trial that followed gave Hitler national attention.

of the eternal court of history will smile and tear up the motions of the state's attorney and the judgment of this court: for she finds us not guilty.

Hitler's Rise to Power

Hitler had to create a distinctive image for the Nazi movement. He could rely upon two major assets—his own popularity as a speaker and the young, dynamic image that the Nazi movement was able to project. This was not to be a normal political organization using old-fashioned methods, but a messianic crusade that could tap the energies and enthusiasm of young German men who were disillusioned with the current political situation. In his memoirs, written in the 1950s, Albert Krebs, at one time the local Nazi Party leader in Hamburg, described the importance of these young activists to the early Nazi movement.

Characteristic of this period was the rapid . . . disappearance of all those leaders and subleaders, except for a few parliamentary representatives, whose attitudes and political methods were still rooted in the prewar era. In their place now stood the young men of the so-called "front line generation," aged twenty-five to thirty-five.

The significance of this changing of the guard can hardly be overestimated. The unquestioning quality of their feelings and judgments, the unweakened power of their belief, the purely physical energy and combativeness of these young men gave the Nazi party a striking power that had to be met sooner or later, especially by the middle-class parties. The assaults of youth are seldom bogged down in the barbed wire of gray experience or the mine fields of skepticism . . . The first to learn this were the racialist groups and parties whose leadership still represented the bypassed conservative, or more properly, reactionary attitudes of the past. Within two short years, by about 1928, they were utterly insignificant in politics, even those which . . . had once had a few hundred thousand members and followers. Even in Hamburg, where the Nazi party developed rather slowly, the Racial Freedom party was in full dissolution within a year. "Without youth you can't organize," one of their representatives told me; "you can't even distribute leaflets."

This German Workers Party membership card reflects one of Hitler's first steps in pursuing a career in politics. However, Hitler was not the seventh member of the party, as this card suggests, and he joined the DAP in January 1920, not in September 1919. Hitler was actually member number 555, but number seven made Hitler seem to be one of the very first to join the new movement.

Between December 1924 and September 1930, the Nazis were never able to win more than 3 percent of the vote in national elections. Hitler's major achievement in these years was simply keeping the movement alive through his ability to convince the Nazi rank and file that they were engaged in a great crusade against Marxism. When the depression hit Germany in 1929, the Nazis had already built up a dedicated army of party activists who could exploit the new electoral opportunities created by the economic crisis. The Nazis invested great energy in their attempts to reach potential voters. In May 1930, a document drawn up by the Prussian Ministry of the Interior described some of the Nazis' tactics.

Selected districts are veritably inundated and worked-over with propaganda operations consisting of methodically and skillfully prepared written and verbal appeals as well as a schedule of meetings, all of which in terms of sheer activity cannot in the least be matched by any other party or political movement.

Hardly a day passes when there are not several meetings held in even very narrowly defined local areas. Carefully organized propaganda headquarters in the individual districts see to it that speakers and topics are in tune with local conditions and economic circumstances... Through systematic training courses, correspondence courses, and recently through the NSDAP [National Socialist German Worker's Party] speaker-training school established on July 1, 1929... agitators are trained for this task over a period of months and even years. If they prove to be qualified they receive official recognition from the party and are given a contract to give at least thirty speeches during an eight-month period, for which they are granted an incentive fee of 20 Reichsmark per evening in addition to expenses.

Rhetorical skills are combined with lecture topics carefully selected to suit the particular audience, which in the rural areas and in small towns is mainly interested in economic matters... Meetings with an audience of between one thousand and five thousand people are a daily occurrence in the bigger cities.... At these events the government's entire internal and foreign policy is attacked in a demagogical style that does not shy away even from falsification, distortion, and slander. They are abusive and contemptuous of the government and blame it for the economic crisis.... This propaganda is backed up almost everywhere by the simultaneous appearance of SA people, who, on bicycles or on trucks—some belonging to the party—go to the individual

Reichsmark

German unit of currency

SA

Short for Sturmabteilung, meaning storm troopers, the political soldiers of the Nazi movement.

A black day for Germany. The Nazis have increased the number of their seats almost tenfold, from 12 to 107, and have become the second strongest party in the Reichstag.

—Count Harry Kessler, diary entry for Monday, September 15, 1930

meetings in an area and merely through being there give a speaker considerable support, help fill the hall itself, act as a protective force for the meeting, and in the end also act as a coercive force in that they allow no one to interject or contradict the speaker, which more or less makes it impossible for anyone to make counterarguments. By their public appearance they directly and indirectly help advertise the meeting, and thereby support the speaker's propaganda, entice sympathizers and the curious, and ultimately through their organization of parades in uniform they win supporters locally, primarily from among the younger generation.

In the mid-1920s, the Nazis had concentrated on winning the urban working-class vote, but with very little success. Then, at the end of the 1920s, the Nazis discovered a new potential constituency—rural Protestant farmers who felt threatened by the power of big industry and organized labor. A 1927 Nazi election leaflet depicts the farmers' economic problems as being the result of a wider, concerted Jewish campaign to take over German wealth and resources.

Farmers, it is a matter of your house and home!
We told you years ago but you didn't listen, just like the rest of the German people. The middle classes should have listened during the years of the insane inflation. Now they have been annihilated: their possessions and savings have been stolen—expropriated!
The German worker expected the revolution to bring honor and beauty into his life. Now he is (to the extent that he can find work) the starving wage-slave of the Bank-Jews.
AND NOW IT'S YOUR TURN GERMAN FARMERS!

Factories, forests, railways, taxes and the state's finances have all been robbed by the Jew. Now he's stretching his greedy fingers towards the last German possession—the German countryside.

You farmer, will be chased from your plot of earth, which you have inherited from your forefathers since time immemorial. Insatiable Jewish race-lust and fanaticism are the driving forces behind this devilish attempt to break Germany's backbone through the annihilation of the German farming community....

Don't you see the vile plan?! The same Jews who control the monopoly on sales of nitrogen, calcium and phosphorus, thereby dictating to you the high price of essential fertilizers, never give you a just price for your produce on the Stock Exchange.

Huge imports of frozen meat and foreign grain, at lowest prices, undercut you and push down your earnings...

And one thing more which is ruining you. You cannot obtain credit to tide you over these hard times. If you want money the usurous interest rates will wring your neck. Under the protection of the state it won't be long before the greater part of the land-owning farmers will be driven from their farms and homes by Jewish money lenders.

The plight of the German farmer is desperate.

Think it all over in your last few hours, and remember—we have been telling you the same thing for years!

Once again we're coming to you. This time you won't laugh at us!

BUT IT'S NEVER TOO LATE!

A people that has the will to live and struggle will survive. Don't stand on the sidelines. Join our struggle against the Jews and loan capital! Help us build a new Germany that will be

NATIONALIST AND SOCIALIST

Nationalist because it is free and held in respect. Socialist because any German who works and creates, will be guaranteed not just a slave's ration of bread, but an honorable life, decent earnings and the sanctity of his hard-earned property. Farmers, it is a matter of the most holy possession of a people,

THE LAND AND THE FIELDS WHICH GOD HAS GIVEN US

Farmers, it is a matter of house and home,

Of life and death,

Of our people and our fatherland!

THEREFORE FARMER—WAKE UP!

Join the ranks of our defence force. Fight with us in the

NATIONAL SOCIALIST GERMAN WORKERS PARTY

Although rural areas initially proved to be the richest source of new Nazi voters, the Nazis did not limit their propaganda efforts to the countryside. In the cities and small towns of Germany many economically distressed artisans, or crafts-people, and small shopkeepers also believed that the Weimar Republic had no answers to their problems. In this leaflet from the late 1920s, the Nazis tried to exploit this alienation from the Weimar "system."

Traders! Small Producers! Artisans!

For a long time you have kept out of sight and let corruption, favouritism and the nepotism of others run all over you. You believed that obeying law and order was the first duty of the citizen.

Nazi Economic Anti-Semitism

The Nazis played on traditional stereotypes of the Jewish moneylender who cheated debtors by demanding exorbitant interest rates. More generally, the Nazis presented Jews as parasites who unfairly extracted money from commercial exchanges without actually doing any work themselves.

helots

A class of serfs, or slaves, in the ancient Greek state of Sparta

But what has this led to? Ever more exploitation by those in power. The tax-screw being turned ever tighter. You are the helots of this system. Your only job is to work and pay taxes which go into the salaries and pensions of ministers.

What have your parties done for you? They promised the world but did nothing. They made coalitions, prattled away before the elections then disappeared into parliament until the next.

They didn't unite against the treacherous leaders of Marxism. They horse dealt over ministerial posts and never gave you a thought.

They have ruled with Social Democrats and forgotten the aim of that party—Death to the Middle Class!

Have you forgotten the inflation? How you were robbed of your savings and commercial capital?

In their attacks on Jews, the Nazis were targeting a very small and quite vulnerable minority in German society. In 1933, when Hitler came to power there were only 505,000 Jews in a total population of 67 million Germans, including those living in the Saar province, on the western border with France, which was still administered by the League of Nations. German Jews made up only 0.75 percent of the total population. More than half of the small number of Jews lived in the ten largest German cities. Berlin was the largest center of Jewish population, with about 160,000 Jews in 1925 or less than 4 percent of the total.

Henry Buxbaum was a German Jew born in 1900 in Assenheim, in the central German province of Hesse. In 1908, his family moved to the city of Friedberg in Upper Hesse. In his memoir, completed in 1979, Buxbaum described life in Germany before and after the First World War.

German First

The great majority of German Jews considered themselves to be fully German. More than 80 percent of all the Jews in Germany had German citizenship. Many had ceased to practice any form of Jewish religious observance and had become either secular, or nonreligious, or had converted to German Protestantism. Some Jewish families had been in Germany for generations. There was a good deal of intermarriage between Jews and non-Jews. In Weimar Germany, Jews played important roles in the German economy and made major contributions to German culture as doctors, lawyers, scientists, businessmen, writers, artists, filmmakers, and actors. More recent and much poorer Jewish immigrants from Poland and Russia found employment at the lower end of the socioeconomic scale, as small traders or manual workers.

The native Friedberger Jews, whose ancestors had been residents in the Jewish quarter of the city for many generations, considered themselves nobility and looked down with contempt and derision at the "yokels," the peasant Jews, who only lately had arrived from the surrounding villages. These old families never fully accepted the newcomers...[who] had not lived there for three hundred years or longer as had some of the older families...

But the real division, and the one which counted most in the daily life of the community, was the difference between rich and poor, between people of wealth and the others of little means, the group to which we belonged. I never was able to overcome my feelings of inferior status within the social life of the community. Not that it mattered with my friends, some of whom belonged to the rich families in town, but it certainly affected me as soon as I entered their houses. As a boy during our earlier years in Friedberg, each time I was invited to a birthday party... I remember with what awe and discomfort I entered such a house...

The time when antisemitic agitation became more than an after-hours entertainment started at the moment of Germany's defeat [in World War I] and the so-called November Revolution. Each segment of German society was severely affected by the two events. But the group which felt the changes more than any other was the German-Jewish community. Suddenly the whole atmosphere of Jewish life inside Germany changed for the worse. You could taste antisemitism everywhere; the air of Germany was permeated by it. All the unavoidable consequences of military defeat, revolution, a ruinous inflation, the Versailles Treaty, the loss of the territories in the east and west, the unsettling social changes following in their wake—each and everything was blamed on the Jews and/or the Communists, who for the convinced Jew-hater were interchangeable...

I was on a train one night on my way home from Frankfurt. The train was pitch-dark. The lights were out, nothing uncommon after the war when the German railroads were in utter disrepair and very few things functioned orderly. It was in either 1919 or 1920, during one of the early periods of violent antisemitic attacks which might occur anywhere, and when a Jew who had the guts to fight could become embroiled in a vicious brawl. It happened often enough on a train and it was difficult not to react to the slander and the smears poured over you. That night, we were seven or eight people in the dark, fourth-class compartment, sitting in utter silence till one of the men started the usual refrain: "Those God-damned Jews, they are at the root of all our troubles." Quickly, some of the others joined in. I couldn't see them and had no idea who they were, but from their voices they sounded like younger men. They sang the same litany over and over again, blaming the Jews for everything that had gone wrong with Germany and for anything else wrong in this world. It went on and on, a cacophony of obscenities, becoming more vicious and at the same time more unbearable with each new sentence echoing in my ears. Finally, I couldn't stand it any longer. I knew very well that to start up with them would get me into trouble, and that to answer them wasn't exactly the height of wisdom, but I couldn't help it. As happened so often during those years when I was confronted with this

Two women confidently declare that "We women are voting for List 2/National Socialist" on this 1932 election poster. The Nazis knew that they could not hope to come to power by winning elections unless they had the support of women voters.

sort of thing, I had to respond to it. I was burning with rage and told them exactly what I thought of them and their vicious talk. I began naturally with the announcement: "Well, I am a Jew and etc., etc." That was the signal they needed. Now they really went after me, threatening me physically. I didn't hold my tongue as the argument went back and forth. They began jostling me till one of them next to me and near the door, probably more encouraged by the darkness than by his own valor, suggested: "Let's throw the Jew out of the train." Now, I didn't dare ignore this signal, and from then on kept quiet. I knew that silence for the moment was better than falling under the wheels of a moving train.

The Rise and Fall of Hitler's Storm Troopers

Without the SA (Sturmabteilung, meaning "storm troopers") Hitler would not have made a significant impact on Weimar politics. The SA was an organization within the Nazi Party made up of paramilitary squads of brownshirts, as they were called because of their brown uniforms. During elections, the SA did most of the grassroots work of campaigning for the Nazi Party. Between elections, the SA kept the Nazi movement in the public eye by marching in formation and engaging in physical fights with Communists. A Nazi Party report, dated February 1927, describes one such battle between Communists and Nazis in a working-class neighborhood of Berlin.

On the 11th of this month the Party held a public mass meeting in the Pharus [Beer] Halls in Wedding, the real working class quarter, with the subject: "The Collapse of the Bourgeois Class State." Comrade Dr. Goebbels was the speaker. It was quite clear to us what that meant. It had to be visibly shown that National Socialism is determined to reach the workers. We succeeded once before in getting a foothold in Wedding. There were huge crowds at the meeting. More than 1,000 people filled the hall whose political composition was four-fifths SA to one-fifth KPD [German Communists]. But the latter had gathered their main forces in the street.

When the meeting was opened by Comrade Daluege, the SA leader, there were, as was expected, provocative shouts of "On a point of order!". After the KPD members had been told that we, not they, decided points of order, and that they would have the right to ask questions after the talk by Comrade Dr. Goebbels, the first scuffling broke out. Peace seemed to be restored until there was renewed heckling. When the chairman announced that the hecklers would be sent out if the interruptions continued, the KPD worked themselves into a frenzy. Meanwhile, the SA had gradually surrounded the center of the disturbance, and the Communists, sensing the danger, suddenly became aggressive.

What followed all happened within three or four minutes. Within seconds both sides had picked up chairs, beer mugs, even tables, and a savage fight began. The Communists were gradually pushed under the gallery which we had taken care to occupy and soon chairs and glasses came hurtling down from there also. The fight was quickly decided: the KPD left with 85 wounded, more or less: that is to say, they could not get down the stairs as fast as they had calmly and "innocently" climbed them. On our side we counted 3 badly wounded and about 10-12 slightly. When the police appeared the fight was already over. Marxist terrorism had been bloodily suppressed.

Nazi storm troopers (SA) beat up their political enemies in the street. In the early 1930s, political violence between communists and Nazis escalated in the streets of Berlin and other German cities.

In early 1933, the aged president of Germany, Paul von Hindenburg, appointed Hitler as chancellor. In his first months in office, Hitler tried to present himself as Hindenburg's responsible partner in promoting a national (not a Nazi) revolution that would make Germany strong again and crush her internal enemies. The first victims of Hitler's revolution were the Communists and the Socialists. (Communists believed in a Russian-style revolution, socialists supported parliamentary democracy and a peaceful evolution toward socialism.) In February, a Dutch anarchist with connections to German communism set fire to the Reichstag (the Parliament building).

The general desire of businessmen was to see a strong man come to power in Germany who would form a government that would stay in power for a long time.

—Report from a meeting at the house of the banker Kurt von Schroeder, Cologne, Germany, January 4, 1933

A starkly simple Nazi election poster reads "Our Last Hope: Hitler." It appealed to the unemployed during the depression, but more unemployed Germans voted for the Communists than for the Nazi party.

The Nazis claimed that the Reichstag fire was the first step in a Communist uprising. Many Communists and Socialists were thrown into concentration camps that had been hastily set up by Hitler's storm troopers. These concentration camps were prisons usually consisting of a set of fenced-in buildings, where political prisoners were kept under armed guard in bad conditions and with no legal rights. In his testimony at the postwar Nuremberg trials, Rudolf Diels, the first head of the Gestapo (Hitler's secret state police), described how these political prisoners were mistreated and sometimes murdered.

The perfectly primitive Nazi conception of the conduct of a state was, that one had to annihilate or render harmless all adversaries or suspected adversaries. The inferiority complex of the Nazis towards everything they did not know, e.g. legal institutions, experts and so on has much to do with that.

As for that, it was a natural matter for the new Nazi Government and the party, which had come into power, to annihilate their adversaries by all possible means. These actions started after the Reichstag fire. They were executed by various party groups, especially by the SA; for such criminal purposes the government also tried to make the most of certain official government agencies. The methods applied were as follows: Human beings... deprived of their freedom [were] subjected to severe bodily mistreatment or killed. These illegal detentions...took place in camps, often old military barracks, storm-troop quarters or fortresses. Later on these places became known as concentration camps, such as Oranienburg, near Berlin, Lichtenberg, Papenburg, Dachau in Bavaria, Columbiahouse Berlin, etc.

During this period of time, numerous politicians, deputies, writers, doctors, lawyers and other personalities of leading circles were arrested illegally, tortured and killed.... These murders were camouflaged by the expression: "shot while trying to escape" or "resisting arrest" or similar things...

There was no legal possibility left any more, to undertake anything in order to stop these illegal arrests, because the Reich Cabinet had suspended Civil Rights by decree of February 28th 1933. On account of this fact, it was also impossible for the inmates of the concentration camps to appeal to any court. Such a state of affairs had never existed before, not even during extraordinary times. The word "protective custody" as used at that time for concentration camps etc. was an irony. There were a few

The SA rounds up political opponents to be sent to the concentration camps in 1933. After Hitler came to power, the first victims of Nazi terror were communists, socialists, and other political enemies of the Nazis.

cases of real protective custody, in which I put people behind safe walls, in order to protect them against terrible excesses.

The SA saw Hitler as the prophet of the New Germany, but his new role as chancellor and partner with Hindenburg made some party members question his dedication to this vision. If the SA men began to suspect that Hitler had only used them to get into power they might revolt. As early as June 1933, the leader of the SA, Ernst Röhm, suggested in a newspaper article that the radical Nazi Revolution the SA expected after Hitler came to power was in danger of being betrayed.

The course of events between 30 January and 21 March 1933 does not represent the sense and meaning of the German National Socialist revolution.

Anyone who wanted to be a fellow-traveler only during shining torchlight processions and impressive parades with rumbling drums and booming kettledrums, with blaring trumpets and under waving flags, and now believes he has "taken part" in the German revolution—can go home! He has confused the "national uprising" with the German revolution! He has intoxicated himself with outward appearances; . . . perhaps he was delighted to see millions and millions of workers march for Germany at the Festival of German Labor, and for a few hours felt a breath of our spirit—but he is not one of us!! For the coming years of struggle he can creep back to

Festival of German Labor

A Nazi celebration of the importance of manual labor, which was supposed to replace the existing socialist May Day

SS

Schutzstaffel, meaning "protective escort." Established in 1925, the original members of the SS were Hitler's personal bodyguards

Asia

Meaning Soviet Communism, which was seen by the Nazis as non-Western, or Asian, and hence extremely dangerous

the hearth or the desk or the pub from whence he came. The fighters in the simple brown service shirt of the SA and SS will not miss him on their path forwards to the German revolution, just as they did not meet him when, in long years marked by sacrifices and blood, they fought their passionate fight for a new Germany. . . .

The SA and SS will not tolerate the German revolution going to sleep or being betrayed at the half-way stage by non-combatants. Not for their own sake, but for Germany's sake. For the brown army is the last levy of the nation, the last bastion against Communism.

If the German revolution is wrecked by reactionary opposition, incompetence, or indolence, the German people will fall into despair and will be an easy prey for the bloodstained frenzy coming from the depths of Asia.

By the beginning of 1934, the SA had 2.4 million members. The army feared that Röhm wanted to make the SA into a military force. The message to Hitler from the military leaders and other influential figures who had helped him become chancellor was clear: tame the SA or risk losing power. This was not a difficult choice for Hitler. The "Night of the Long Knives" (a typical Nazi euphemism, in this case for the murder of almost two hundred people) was carried out on June 30, 1934, by Heinrich Himmler's black-shirted SS. The SS, originally made up of Hitler's personal bodyguards, was under the organizational control of the SA, until this bloody changing of the guard. To justify this violent purge, Hitler claimed that the SA was planning an uprising. In his 1969 memoir, Hitler's favorite architect, Albert Speer, described his reactions to the news that the SA leadership had been executed.

I was in Berlin. . . Tension hung over the city. Soldiers in battle array were encamped in the Tiergarten [an area of Berlin]. Trucks full of police holding rifles cruised the streets. There was clearly an air of "something cooking," . . .

Late on the morning of July 1, Hitler returned after making a series of arrests in Munich, and I received a telephone call from his adjutant; "Have you any new designs? If so, bring them here!" That suggested that Hitler's entourage was trying to distract him by turning his mind to his architectural interests . . .

His entourage tried to deepen his distaste for the executed SA leaders by assiduously reporting as many details as possible about the intimate life of Roehm [Röhm] and his following. Bruckner showed Hitler the menus of banquets held by the Roehm clique, which had purportedly been found in the Berlin SA headquarters. The menus listed a fantastic variety of courses, including foreign delicacies such as frogs' legs, birds' tongues, shark fins, seagulls' eggs, along with vintage French wines and the best champagnes. Hitler commented sarcastically: "So, here we have those revolutionaries! And our revolution was too tame for them.". . .

The leadership became frenziedly busy justifying the operation. A day of great activity ended with a speech by Hitler to a special session of the Reichstag. His feelings of guilt were audible in his protestations of innocence. A Hitler defending himself was something we would not encounter again in the future, not even in 1939, at the beginning of the war. . . what most impressed me, as well as many of my unpolitical acquaintances, was the attitude of Hindenburg. The field marshal of the First World War was held in reverence by people of middle-class origins. Even in my school days he epitomized the strong, steadfast hero of modern history, and as such seemed to belong to a somewhat legendary realm. . . That Hitler's action was approved by this supreme judge was highly reassuring.

It was no accident that after the Roehm putsch the Right, represented by the President, the Minister of Justice, and the generals, lined up behind Hitler. . . Their conservatism had nothing in common with racist delusions. Their open display of sympathy for Hitler's intervention sprang from quite different causes: in the Blood Purge of June 30, 1934, the strong left wing of the party, represented chiefly by the SA, was eliminated. That wing had felt cheated of the fruits of the revolution. And not without reason. For the majority of the members of the SA, raised in the spirit of revolution before 1933, had taken Hitler's supposedly socialist program seriously. During my brief period of activity in Wannsee I had been able to observe, on the lowest plane, how the ordinary SA man sacrificed himself for the movement, giving up time and personal safety in the expectation that he would some day receive tangible compensation. When nothing came of that, anger and discontent built up. It could easily have reached the explosive point. Possibly Hitler's action did indeed avert that "second revolution" Roehm was supposed to have been plotting.

With such arguments we soothed our consciences. I myself and many others snatched avidly at excuses; the things that would have offended us two years before we now accepted as the standard of our new environment. Any troublesome doubts were repressed.

Captain Ernst Röhm, head of the SA and one of Hitler's oldest and closest political colleagues. Hitler had him and other SA leaders murdered in 1934.

Wannsee

An upper-middle-class residential neighborhood of Berlin.

Chapter Three: Picture Essay

Selling Hitler's Image
Nazi Propaganda

In the 1920s, for the first time, modern visual media began to exert a powerful influence on the way millions of Germans understood their world. Advertising, magazines, and movies engulfed Germans in a flood of pictures. The Nazis recognized the value of this new world of images and they quickly learned how to use visual propaganda in their fights to win elections. After 1933, the Nazis monopolized the production of images, at least within Germany, and, after 1939, in German-occupied territories. A well-known German film director insisted after the war that few of the images produced under Nazism could be trusted, that all were in some way propaganda. What he meant is quite clear if we look at graphic art, posters, or many of the paintings of the Third Reich. Even photographs could be staged to present a specific point of view.

Hitler was at the center of Nazi visual propaganda. Pictures of Hitler appeared on stamps, postcards, and in booklets. Hitler was on billboards. Hitler was in the newsreels. Framed photos of Hitler were given as Christmas gifts. In 1936, Hitler's image was projected every evening onto the façade of Munich's city hall. This visual assault was part of a larger attempt to create a public image of Hitler, a Hitler myth, which was often the very opposite of his real self. This Hitler myth raised him out of the ranks of ordinary politicians and gave him a special authority and popularity unlike any other German leader before him.

After 1933, more and more Germans, even those who had never voted for Hitler, came to regard the Führer as the embodiment of the nation and the guardian of the unity of the "national community" above all selfish sectional interest. Millions of Germans credited him with pulling Germany out of the Great Depression. He was also seen as the representative of popular justice, a great statesman, a military genius, and as a bulwark against the nation's political and racial enemies—the Marxists and the Jews. In constructing this Hitler myth, pictures proved to be every bit as powerful as words.

Hitler's portrait is displayed in a Mercedes automobile showroom in Munich in 1935. From the early days of the Nazi movement, Hitler traveled in a large, open Mercedes. After Hitler came to power, Mercedes hoped to cash in on the long-standing association in the public mind between Hitler and the car company. The message is: Buy a Mercedes and you will be driving the Führer's car.

Hitler appears in uniform on this postage stamp, which was produced for the 1939 Nuremberg Party rally. Hitler regarded his Nazi movement as a sort of religious crusade against Germany's enemies. Many in the audience would have seen the Hitler who appears here as a prophet delivering a sermon rather than merely a politician.

In the dark days after Germany had been defeated and forced to accept a humiliating peace, the Nazis tried to show that their movement was Germany's only chance to return to greatness. And only an ordinary person, a man like Hitler, could unite Germany. When Heinrich Hoffmann learned from Hitler that he had been in the crowd gathered in a Munich public square to celebrate the start of World War I, the photographer spent hours going over his picture of the event with a magnifying glass until he found Hitler's face. Hoffmann then enlarged this part of the photo and pasted it onto the original to demonstrate that Hitler had been part of the "August experience" of national unity and pride in Germany.

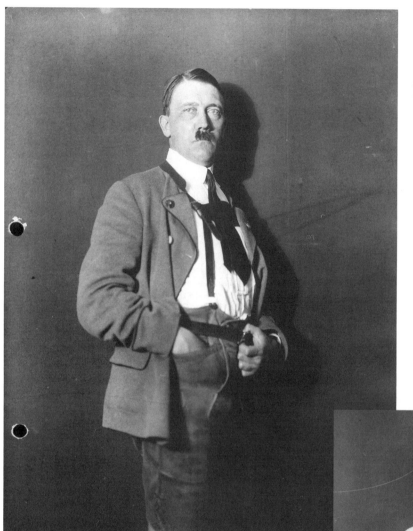

Hitler and his personal photographer, Heinrich Hoffmann, worked together to present exactly the right image of Hitler to the German public. In 1925–26 Hitler tried the same pose in two different types of clothing. On the left, Hitler is dressed in a traditional Bavarian costume, complete with leather shorts.

Though the image above might have pleased conservative Bavarians, it was rejected in favor of the one on right, which perhaps had a broader appeal.

Hitler preferred to be photographed in militaristic uniforms, which he had himself designed. In this carefully staged photograph taken in February 1933, Hitler leads strong and determined young German males, who are also dressed in military uniform, to a better future.

Es lebe Deutschland!

Party members often saw the Nazi movement as a religious crusade to save Germany from communism. Hitler was presented as a Christ-like prophet. Some of the party faithful even made direct comparisons between Jesus Christ and Hitler, drawing intense criticism from Christian leaders in Germany. This poster, produced sometime after 1936, is one of the more extreme uses of Christian imagery by Nazi propagandists. When John the Baptist baptized Christ, a dove descended from the sky. Here, instead, an eagle appears to be flying toward Hitler. The caption reads: "Long Live Germany."

In September 1933, Hitler breaks ground for the construction of the new German freeway (autobahn) system in Frankfurt am Main, reminding Germans that he was personally responsible for this great new national project, and for putting Germany back to work after the massive unemployment and despair of the Great Depression. The picture also presents Hitler as a man of the people, unafraid to dirty his hands with manual labor.

The technique of photomontage (literally mounting or pasting together different parts of separate photographs) allowed Hitler's supporters to make strong visual arguments that could not be presented with just one original photograph. The picture of Hitler digging was pasted together with two other photographs of the new armies of German workers set in motion by Hitler's new Nazi regime, suggesting that these newly employed men would work with the Führer to rebuild Germany and make it strong. The poster's caption reads "The army of labor and of peace responds to the Führer with a [resounding] Yes!"

Jur hiftorifchen Begegnung   29. Septbr. 1938 in München

This German postcard was issued "On the occasion of a historic meeting, 29 September 1938 in Munich." It celebrates Hitler's triumph at the conference where, in order to prevent a war, England and France gave Germany the Sudetenland, the ethnic-German western border area of Czechoslovakia. Images of Hitler and Mussolini, the dictator of Italy and Hitler's ally, face representatives of the great powers: England's Neville Chamberlain (left) and France's Edouard Daladier (center). Hitler's association with these powerful men suggests he is a formidable statesman who has enabled Germany to regain its status as a great power.

By the early 1930s, Hoffmann had realized that he needed to soften Hitler's image or at least to present another more "human" side of the Nazi Party leader. He did this by presenting Hitler in homely and informal poses. In a typically sentimental image of the private Hitler, the man eventually responsible for the deaths of millions of European children, takes a moment to pose with some young "friends."

This picture of a smiling Hitler greeting jubilant German soldiers in 1941 appears to be a candid photograph documenting a spontaneous moment. But photography—like other forms of visual media—was controlled by the Nazi state. Photographs like this one were taken by members of official army propaganda companies. The pictures were circulated in Nazi publications to create an image of Hitler as victorious general who had erased the shame of German defeat in World War I.

Burning wooden barracks in the Bergen-Belsen concentration camp on which the Nazis had draped a portrait of Hitler. The end of the war also meant the end of the Holocaust. When British forces liberated Bergen-Belsen on April 15, 1945, they found 60,000 prisoners, most of them very ill. After evacuating the camp, the British burned the barracks to prevent the spread of disease.

Chapter Four

The Racial State

Nazi Germany, 1933–1939

Race was at the center of the Nazi worldview. The Nazis believed that the biological makeup of a country determined its destiny, and Germany would have to be purified of all non-Aryan elements in order to survive and to become powerful. Hitler insisted that Germany's main racial enemy—the Jews—had already begun to take over and seriously weaken the country. According to the Nazis, an international Jewish conspiracy was responsible for Germany's defeat in World War I, for the German revolution of 1918–1919, and for the threat of communism. The Nazis believed that Jews were a different race than Aryan Germans, and that the economic, cultural, and political lives and values of Jews and Aryan Germans were determined by their very different and quite incompatible biological natures. In Hitler's eyes, Jews could never become Aryan Germans because each of the two races had different and opposed "blood," or what we might call genetic makeup.

Hitler felt that a long list of other biologically defined groups also posed important threats to the future health and strength of the Aryan German race. This list included even other Aryan Germans if they were thought to be biologically deficient. The Nazis believed that Germans suffering from a wide range of mental and physical disabilities imposed an intolerable burden on the healthy majority of the population. The deficient genes that were assumed to be responsible for these physical or mental handicaps would no longer be allowed to circulate in the larger German gene pool. At the very least, these "ballast existences" and "useless eaters"—common Nazi descriptions of Aryan Germans considered to have mental or physical disabilities—should not be allowed to reproduce.

The Nazis realized that if they wanted to construct a racial state they would have to do more than discriminate against, exclude, and

An SA man stands guard outside a store to scare away customers during the April 1933 Nazi-sponsored boycott of Jewish-owned businesses. The sign reads: "Germans defend yourselves! Don't buy from Jews!"

persecute minorities they considered to be racially dangerous or biologically unfit. The millions of Germans whom the Nazis regarded as biologically valuable would have to be convinced that they were members of a single racial community, not merely workers or industrialists, Protestants or Catholics. Hitler wanted to recreate the intense sense of national unity that the Germans had experienced during the First World War, but he wanted Aryan Germans to realize that they were now fighting in a different kind of war, a life and death racial struggle against their biological enemies. The Aryan German race would either defeat its enemies and become the racial master of Europe or it would be destroyed. Hitler believed that this racial struggle would inevitably lead to a new world war. To achieve victory, Germans would have to be united as never before.

Making German Jews and "Community Aliens" Socially Dead

When Hitler came to power, he could not simply kill all the German Jews right away. Anti-Semitism was widespread in German society, but most ordinary Germans were not prepared, in 1933, to accept mass murder. So, the Nazis had to see just how far they could go without creating significant resistance. They began by making German Jews socially dead. This meant stripping them of their legal rights as citizens and forcing them out of the professions in which they worked. It also involved reaching into private lives by, for example, forbidding any future marriages between Jewish and non-Jewish Germans. In 1935, the Nazis issued the Nuremberg Laws (The Reich Citizenship Law and the Law for the Protection of German Blood and Honor), which officially segregated Jews from non-Jews.

The Reich Citizenship Law of September 15, 1935
...ARTICLE 2. (1) A citizen of the Reich may be only one who is of German or kindred blood, and who, through his behavior, shows that he is both desirous and personally fit to serve loyally the German people and the Reich...

First Supplementary Decree of November 14, 1935
...ARTICLE 4. (1) A Jew cannot be a citizen of the Reich. He cannot exercise the right to vote; he cannot occupy public office. (2) Jewish officials will be retired as of December 31, 1935...

The "Eternal Jew Exhibition," which opened in Munich in 1937, tried to convince Germans that Jews were the number-one racial enemy. The exhibit promoted Nazi stereotypes of Jews, such as the figure in this postcard, who holds gold coins in his right hand; anti-Semites believed Jews controlled banks and stock markets. In his left hand, the man has a whip, and in the crook of his arm rests a map of the Soviet Union; two symbols representing the anti-Semitic belief that Jews had enslaved the Russian people by starting the Russian Revolution, which brought the communists to power in that country.

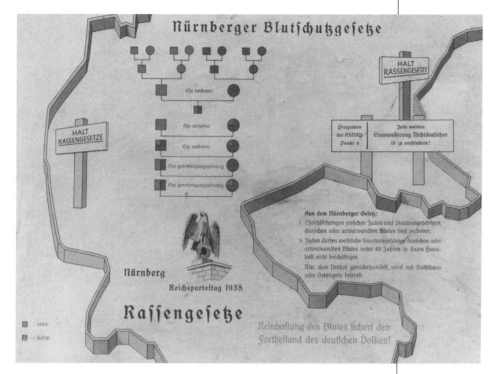

A Nazi poster lays out the prohibited degrees of marriage between Aryans and non-Aryans, according to the 1935 Nuremberg Race Laws. The German text reads "Maintaining the purity of blood insures the survival of the German people."

ARTICLE 5. (1) A Jew is an individual who is descended from at least three grandparents who were, racially, full Jews...

(2) A Jew is also an individual who is descended from two full-Jewish grandparents if:

(a) he was a member of the Jewish religious community when this law was issued, or joined the community later;

(b) when the law was issued, he was married to a person who was a Jew, or was subsequently married to a Jew;

(c) he is the issue from a marriage with a Jew, in the sense of Section I, which was contracted after the coming into effect of the Law for the Protection of German Blood and Honor of September 15, 1935;

(d) he is the issue of an extramarital relationship with a Jew, according to Section I, and born out of wedlock after July 31, 1936...

The Law for the Protection of German Blood and Honor, September 15, 1935

...ARTICLE 1. (1) Any marriages between Jews and citizens of German or kindred blood are herewith forbidden. Marriages entered into despite this law are invalid, even if they are arranged abroad as a means of circumventing this law...

ARTICLE 2. Extramarital relations between Jews and citizens of German or kindred blood are herewith forbidden.

"May 23, Monday [1938] Frau Lehmann appeared on Thursday evening. She had been summoned to an official: It was known that she was a cleaner for a Jewish professor and a Jewish lawyer.—She was over 46, therefore permitted.—'Certainly, but your son will not get his promotion in the Labor Service, and your daughter... will lose her post, if you do not give up this work.'—So the woman was rid of two of her three jobs, and we are alone. On Friday we washed dishes for almost three hours, and our travel plans were abandoned, since house and tomcat cannot be left alone. Frau Lehmann was in our service for eleven years."

—Victor Klemperer, a Jewish protestor who survived the Nazi period because he was married to an Aryan-German woman, in his memoir, *I Will Bear Witness, 1933–44.*

ARTICLE 3. Jews are forbidden to employ as servants in their households female subjects of German or kindred blood who are under the age of forty-five years.

ARTICLE 4. (1) Jews are prohibited from displaying the Reich and national flag and from showing the national colors.

(2) However, they may display the Jewish colors. The exercise of this right is under state protection.

ARTICLE 5. (1) Anyone who acts contrary to the prohibition noted in Article 1 renders himself liable to penal servitude.

(2) The man who acts contrary to the prohibition of Article 2 will be punished by sentence to either a jail or penitentiary.

(3) Anyone who acts contrary to the provisions of Articles 3 and 4 will be punished with a jail sentence up to a year and with a fine, or with one of these penalties.

Because racism was now the law of the land, Aryan Germans could discriminate against Jews without fear of being held to account by the justice system. In August 1935, the town council of the Bernkastel district, in the Rhineland, passed a resolution making it clear that Jews were not welcome in this municipality.

Judaism, which has brought such misfortune on our German Fatherland, is today once again rearing its head more boldly than ever. These parasites on the German body politic underestimate our sense of decency and are again making themselves at home within National Socialist Germany, which they hate so much, and are again pouring out their Jewish impudence and vulgarity.

In recognizing this situation, we have resolved to act accordingly:

- All city exits will be fitted with signs bearing the inscription: JEWS NOT WANTED HERE.
- The journal *Der Stürmer* [the hotspur], on display in the newspaper display box in the town center, will be recommended to all citizens.
- No craftsman, businessman, or any other countryman will receive work contracts from the community and will immediately forfeit entitlement to the use and enjoyment of communal property if he or members of his family continue to traffic with Jews; that is, if he supports their businesses.
- Making purchases from Jews, employing Jewish physicians or lawyers is tantamount to committing a traitorous act against the German people and nation.

An advertisement for the anti-Semitic tabloid Der Stürmer *(the hotspur) presents a crude caricature of a Jew arriving in Germany from eastern Europe. The caption at the bottom insists that "Without a solution to the Jewish question, there can be no redemption of humanity."*

A Jewish woman sitting on a park bench designated for Jews hides her face from the camera. By the end of the 1930s, the Nazis had created a kind of racial apartheid system, which reserved some public spaces only for Aryans and others only for Jews.

- Given the fact that the race question holds the key to our freedom, those who break these fundamental principles are to be scorned and outlawed.

The Nazis believed that during the Weimar Republic Jewish influence had poisoned art, music, and literature. In 1937, the Nazis opened an exhibition in Munich that displayed 650 works of art that they considered "degenerate." After several hundred thousand visitors had attended this Exhibition of Degenerate Art, all these art works and many more that were considered similarly corrupt were removed from German museums and either sold abroad or destroyed. Directly across the street from the Exhibition, Hitler constructed a new House of German Art for work that Hitler and the Nazis thought represented the new spirit of an Aryan Germany. In his speech made at the opening of the House of German Art in July 1937, Hitler made it quite clear what kind of art would no longer be tolerated in Germany.

People have attempted to recommend modern art by saying that it is the expression of a new age: but art does not create a new age, it is the general life of peoples which fashions itself anew and therefore often seeks after a new expression....It is...impudent effrontery...to exhibit to the folk of to-day works which perhaps ten or twenty thousand years ago might have been made by a man of the Stone Age....The new age of today is at work on a new human type. Men and women are to be more healthy, stronger: there is a new feeling of life, a new joy in life....This, my good

A painting by the Jewish artist Marc Chagall depicts the Jewish festival of Purim in a Russian town. The Nazis removed from German museums this and many other paintings they considered to be "degenerate," simply because of their style and subjects.

prehistoric art-stutterers, is the type of the age: and what do you manufacture? Misformed cripples and cretins, women who inspire only disgust, men who are more like wild beasts, children who, were they alive, must be regarded as cursed of God. And let no one say to me that this is how these artists see things . . . it is clear that the eye of some men shows them things otherwise than as they are—that there really are men who on principle feel meadows to be blue, the heaven green, clouds sulphur-yellow—or as they perhaps prefer to say "experience" them thus.

I need not ask whether they really do see or feel things in this way, but in the name of the German people I have only to prevent these pitiable unfortunates who clearly suffer from defects of vision from attempting with violence to persuade contemporaries by their chatter that these faults of observation are indeed realities or from presenting them as "Art." Here only two possibilities are open: either these "artists" do really see things in this way and believe in that which they represent—then one has but to ask how the defect in vision arose, and if it is hereditary the Minister for the Interior will have to see to it that so ghastly a defect of vision shall not be allowed to perpetuate itself—or if they do not believe in the reality of such impressions but seek on other grounds to impose upon the nation by this humbug, then it is a matter for a criminal court.

Jews were not the only victims of Nazi racial persecution. Although there were very few Afro-Germans in Hitler's Third Reich, they too were subjected to discrimination. Hans Massaquoi was the son of a German mother and an African father from a diplomatic family. In his memoir, published in 1999, he describes an encounter with Nazi racism in a park in Hamburg.

As I had done many times before, I had gone to the playground after school for an afternoon of innocent play. My favorite attraction, like everybody else's, was the seesaw, which meant that there was always a waiting line. After patiently awaiting our turn, a boy and I were about to mount when a mother with her young son in tow blocked my way. "Where do you think you are going?" she inquired, her voice shrill with aggravation...

"It's my turn," I said in feeble protest.

"What do you mean 'my turn'?"... You aren't even supposed to be in this playground. Can't you read?" With that, she pointed to a painted sign near the playground's entrance that I had never noticed before...

Thoroughly embarrassed and crushed, I walked away. Before leaving the playground, I studied the sign with eyes blurred with suppressed tears. The sign read:

NICHTARIERN IST DAS BETRETEN DIESES
SPIELPLATZES STRENGSTENS VERBOTEN
(Non-Aryans are sternly prohibited from
entering this playground)

Although I had heard the term *non-Aryan* before, I never felt that it had anything to do with me...

That evening after my mother had returned from work, I pointedly asked her, "Am I a non-Aryan?"

Taken totally by surprise, Mutti [mother] demanded to know what prompted my question. When I told her what had happened on the playground, she conceded that Africans were among several racial groups that had been classified non-Aryans by the Nazi government.

"Since your father is African and you are his son," she explained, "you, too, are classified non-Aryan."

"Are you a non-Aryan, too?" I kept pressing.

"No, I'm not."

"Why not?"

"Because I'm not African; I am European."

"Then why am I a non-Aryan because I'm Dad's son and not an Aryan like you when I'm your son also?" I tried to reason with her...

"I agree that it doesn't make any sense," Mutti conceded. "Tomorrow I'll speak to the park warden. I'm sure he'll make an exception and let you play in the park."

"I don't want you to talk to the warden," I told her. "I don't ever want to play in that park again."

Despite my protest, my mother did have a talk with the warden and he told her that I shouldn't pay any attention to the sign. But nothing Mutti said could make me break my vow never to set foot in that park again.

The Nazis also considered Sinti and Roma, who were commonly referred to as "Gypsies," to be "racially inferior." The Roma had come to Europe from the Punjab region of northern India as nomads between the eighth and tenth centuries. They were called Gypsies because Europeans mistakenly

A propaganda slide, which may have been part of a lecture given by the SS, criticizes a friendship between an Aryan woman and a black woman. The caption reads: "The Result! Racial pride wanes."

The Gypsy is and remains a parasite on the people who supports himself almost exclusively by begging and stealing . . . The Gypsy can never be educated to become a useful person. For this reason it is necessary that the Gypsy tribe be exterminated . . . by way of sterilization or castration.

—Chief of police in the rural district of Esslingen, South Germany, in a letter to the chief administrative officer, 1937

believed they had come from Egypt. Most of the Roma in Germany belonged to the Sinti and Roma family groupings and spoke dialects of a common language called Romani, based on the classical language of India, Sanskrit. Many Germans believed that Roma were by nature dirty, dangerous, and criminal. In December 1938, Heinrich Himmler, head of the much-feared SS, issued a memorandum on the "Fight against the Gypsy Nuisance."

Experience gained in the fight against the Gypsy nuisance, and knowledge derived from race-biological research, have shown that the proper method of attacking the Gypsy problem seems to be to treat it as a matter of race. Experience shows that part-Gypsies play the greatest role in Gypsy criminality. On the other hand, it has been shown that efforts to make the Gypsies settle have been unsuccessful, especially in the case of pure Gypsies, on account of their strong compulsion to wander. It has therefore become necessary to distinguish between pure and part-Gypsies in the final solution of the Gypsy question.

To this end, it is necessary to establish the racial affinity of every Gypsy living in Germany and of every vagrant living a Gypsy-like existence . . .

The police authorities will report (via the responsible Criminal Police offices and local offices) to the Reich Criminal Police Office–Reich Central Office for the Fight against the Gypsy Nuisance all persons who by virtue of their looks and appearance, customs or habits, are to be regarded as Gypsies or part-Gypsies.

Because a person considered to be a Gypsy or part-Gypsy, or a person living like a Gypsy, as a rule confirms the suspicion that marriage (in accordance with clause 6 of the first decree on the implementation of the Law for the Protection of German Blood and Honour . . . or on the basis of stipulations in the law on Fitness to Marry) must not be contracted, in all cases the public registry officials must demand a testimony of fitness to marry from those who make such an application [to be married].

The Nazis also persecuted gay men on racial grounds. The Nazis believed that healthy Aryan males were committing a crime against the Aryan race by not having children, particularly because the heavy casualties of World War I had created a "shortage" of men. Lesbians usually had to hide their homosexuality but were generally not persecuted in the same ways as gay men, because the Nazis saw them as less

of a direct threat to the reproduction of the Aryan race. In February 1937, Himmler gave a speech to SS leaders on the dangers of male homosexuality.

If you... take into account the facts I have not yet mentioned, namely that with a static number of women, we have two million men too few on account of those who fell in the war, then you can well imagine how this imbalance of two million homosexuals and two million war dead, or in other words a lack of about four million men capable of having sex, has upset the sexual balance sheet of Germany, and will result in a catastrophe.

... There are those homosexuals who take the view: what I do is my business, a purely private matter. However, all things which take place in the sexual sphere are not the private affair of the individual, but signify the life and death of the nation... The people which has many children has the candidature for world power and world domination. A people of good race which has too few children has a one-way ticket to the grave, for insignificance in fifty or a hundred years, for burial in two hundred and fifty years...

Therefore we must be absolutely clear that if we continue to have this burden in Germany, without being able to fight it, then that is the end of Germany, and the end of the Germanic world... In the SS, today, we still have about one case of homosexuality a month. In a whole year, about eight to ten cases occur in the entire SS. I have now decided upon the following: in each case, these people will naturally be publicly degraded, expelled, and handed over to the courts. Following completion of the punishment imposed by the courts, they will be sent, by my order, to a concentration camp, and they will be shot in the concentration camp, while attempting to escape. I will make that known by order to the unit to which the person so affected belonged. Thereby, I hope finally to have done with persons of this type in the SS, so that at least the good blood, which we have in the SS, and the increasingly healthy blood which we are cultivating for Germany, will be kept pure.

However this does not represent a solution to the problem for the whole of Germany. One must not have any illusions about the following. When I bring a

A Nazi chart claims to document hereditary criminality and alcoholism in a so-called "criminal family." The Nazis believed that a wide range of social problems were caused by "bad genes."

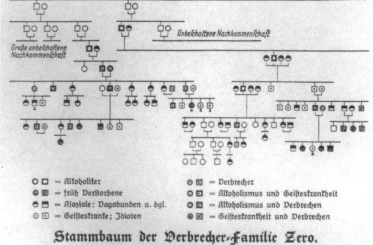

homosexual before the courts and have him locked up, the matter is not settled, because the homosexual comes out of prison just as homosexual as before he went in. Therefore the whole question is not clarified. It is clarified in the sense that this burden has been identified, in contrast to the years before the seizure of power.

After 1933, men who were openly gay found themselves vulnerable to Nazi persecution. In a postwar interview, Harry Pauly, an apprentice hairdresser involved in the theater world, described his experience in Berlin.

When the Nazis came to power, they closed the gay bars. Some homosexuals, especially those who were Jewish, were killed by Nazi hooligans; my friend "Susi," a drag queen, was stabbed to

In 1938, police took this photograph of a Berlin bar that they suspected was a meeting place for gay men. After Hitler came to power, gay men who continued to meet in public were often placed under surveillance by the special section of the Gestapo that dealt with homosexuals. The police wrote notes around the edges of the photograph that describe the bar's location.

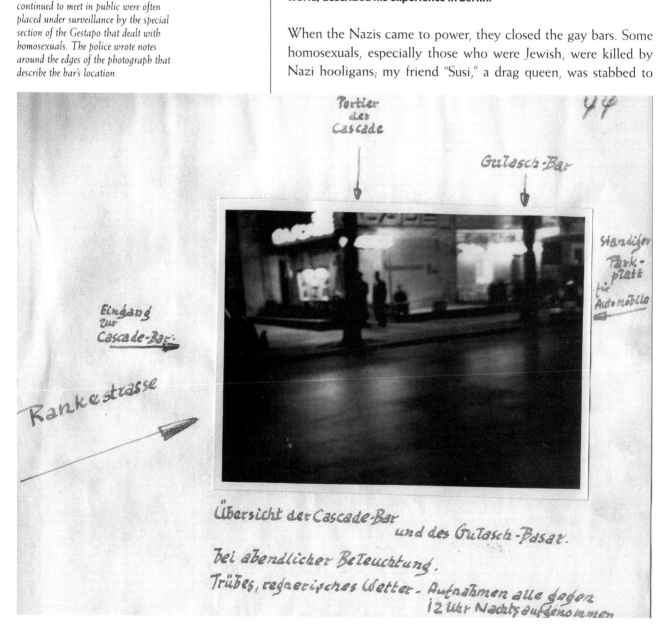

death. In 1936 I was arrested under the Nazi-revised paragraph 175 of the criminal code, which outlawed homosexuality. I was imprisoned in a camp at Neusustrum, where I worked in the marshes 12 hours a day. After 15 months I was released.

Kristallnacht

In November 1938, the Nazis unleashed a massive wave of violence against German Jews. SA men smashed the shop windows of some 7,500 Jewish-owned businesses across Germany, Austria (recently annexed by Hitler), and the Nazi-occupied western Sudetenland region of Czechoslovakia. The shards of broken glass from these windows gave the event its name, *Kristallnacht,* or "The night of broken glass."

Jewish businesses and homes were looted and synagogues burned. *Kristallnacht* erupted shortly after Herschel Grynszpan, a seventeen-year-old Polish Jew, shot Ernst vom Rath, a low-ranking German embassy official, in Paris, on November 7. The Nazis had deported Grynszpan's parents and sister to Poland. In retaliation for the mistreatment of his family, Grynszpan shot vom Rath. On November 12, Reich propaganda minister Goebbels claimed in a newspaper article that the shooting was the work of a "World Jewish Conspiracy" that wanted to destroy Germany.

The questions arise: Where was Grynszpan during the last three months? Who took care of his living expenses? Who gave him the false passport? Who trained him in pistol-shooting? There can be no doubt that he was given sanctuary by a Jewish organization, nor that he was systematically prepared for this cynical assassination...

For some weeks and months now a veritable war has been waged against Germany as a nation by the Jewish world press... The reasons... are obvious. World Jewry, after its feverish incitement to war during the summer months of this year, has undergone a terrible reversal. The Munich Agreement reduced to a shambles its plan to destroy Germany. It had hoped through its infamous incitement to world war to bring Germany to her knees and to bring about the fall of the hated Nazi regime. After its plan was shattered at Munich, it wanted to take drastic and indecent action to halt the efforts for peace between the Great Powers of Europe in order to set the scene for a renewed hate campaign against Germany.

The murder of Legation Secretary vom Rath was to be a beacon for all Jewry in its battle against Germany. The murderer him-

The Nazi newspaper The People's Observer *tries to convince its readers that Herschel Grynszpan's shooting of a German embassy official in Paris is part of a larger Jewish conspiracy. The first part of the headline, which reads "A New Gustloff case," connects the shooting in Paris to an earlier incident in which a Jewish student shot Wilhelm Gustloff, a leader of the foreign organization of the Nazi movement in Switzerland. The rest of the headline reads: "Murderous Jewish Attack in Paris. Member of the German Embassy mortally wounded by shots."*

Munich Agreement

September 1938 agreement between Germany, Italy, Britain, and France, which gave Nazi Germany the German-speaking Sudetenland region of Czechoslovakia.

self confessed that he wanted to give a warning signal by his act. However, this shot went astray. The world was not warned so much as the German people themselves.

Nazi propaganda depicted *Kristallnacht* as a spontaneous explosion of public outrage. In reality, most of the violence was the work of SA men and Nazi Party officials, sometimes dressed in civilian clothes. According to reports in the November 11, 1938, *New York Times*, ordinary Germans displayed mixed reactions to the destruction of Jewish property.

A man sweeps up the broken glass from a Jewish shop window after the event that came to be known as Kristallnacht. *The attacks on Jews that swept across Germany in early November 1938 caused many German Jews to realize that it was time to leave their homeland.*

Crowds Mostly Silent

Generally the crowds were silent and the majority seemed gravely disturbed by the proceedings. Only members of the wrecking squads shouted occasionally, "Perish Jewry!" and "Kill the Jews!" and in one case a person in the crowd shouted, "Why not hang the owner in the window?"

In one case on the Kurfuerstendamm [a major shopping street in Berlin] actual violence was observed by an American girl who saw one Jew with his face bandaged dragged from a shop, beaten and chased by a crowd while a second Jew was dragged from the same shop by a single man who beat him as the crowd looked on.

One Jewish shopowner, arriving at his wrecked store, exclaimed, "Terrible," and was arrested on the spot.

In some cases on the other hand crowds were observed making passages for Jews to leave their stores unmolested.

Some persons in the crowds—peculiarly enough, mostly women—expressed the view that it was only right that the Jews should suffer what the Germans suffered in 1918. But there were also men and women who expressed protests...One man—obviously a worker—watching the burning of a synagogue in the Fasanenstrasse [a street in Berlin], exclaimed, "Arson remains arson." The protestors, however, were quickly silenced by the wrecking crews with threats of violence.

A crowd watches a synagogue burn in Essen, Germany, during the nationwide attacks on Jews in November 1938. Across the country, fire departments were given orders not to take action unless the fires threatened Aryan property.

Warned against Looting

To some extent—at least during the day—efforts were made to prevent looting. Crowds were warned they might destroy but not plunder, and in individual cases looters were either beaten up on the spot by uniformed Nazis or arrested. But for the most part, looting was general, particularly during the night and in the poorer quarters. And at least in one case the wreckers themselves tossed goods out to the crowd with the shout "Here are some cheap Christmas presents."

Children were observed with their mouths smeared with candy from wrecked candy shops or flaunting toys from wrecked toy shops until one elderly woman watching the spectacle exclaimed, "So that is how they teach our children to steal."...

Children "Fish" for Loot

...Before one Friedrichstrasse shop devoted to the sale of magic apparatus children lined up with brass poles that had hooks at the ends. With these they fished magicians' boxes of tricks for themselves out of the interior of the shop through a broken store window.

Older boys unconcernedly threw tables, chairs and other furniture out of smashed windows. One group moved a piano from a shop into the street and played popular tunes for onlookers. Before synagogues, demonstrators stood with Jewish prayer books from which they tore leaves as souvenirs for the crowds. . . .

In connection with *Kristallnacht*, the Nazis sent more than twenty-five thousand Jewish men to Dachau, Buchenwald, and Sachsenhausen concentration camps. Most were released only after they began the process of emigrating from Germany and selling off their property at bargain rates to Aryan Germans, a process that was called Aryanization. Hans Berger was a German Jew who grew up in Wiesbaden, a central German city on the Rhine River. On November 11, he was arrested and sent to Buchenwald concentration camp, near the city of Weimar. After he was allowed to leave the camp, Berger fled to Belgium where he wrote a memoir in which he described his experience of *Kristallnacht* and its aftermath.

Jews arrested during Kristallnacht *assemble for roll call at Buchenwald concentration camp.* Kristallnacht *marked the first time that the Nazis sent large numbers of Jews to concentration camps.*

When on the morning of the 10th of November I was driving my car to work, as I did every day, my route took me past the synagogue, whose dome was ablaze. Fear went right through me. A big crowd of people stood around it silently and the fire department was content with protecting the surrounding houses from catching fire.... The next morning I began my work early and took care of the most urgent business matters... Toward 12:30 two officials of the Gestapo appeared... after a short house search in my office Karl Seibel Jr. drove us together with the two men from the Stapo [state police]... to my residence... There I was given time to change clothes and to take along a few necessary items of clothing... then the men drove me in my own car, with my wife accompanying me, to the court prison... In the evening we were transferred to the police prison... On the next day, Saturday, November 11th, there followed, among other things, an interrogation... about our emigration plans, and Ernst Springer, who in his pocket had his completed ship documents for emigration to America for the 7th of December, was released immediately...

Still on the same evening, in severe cold, we were taken in trucks to Frankfurt to the Festhalle [festival hall], where we arrived at eleven at night. A howling mob received us at the entrance to the Festhalle—abusive shouts, stone-throwing, in short the atmosphere of a pogrom. On the double we went into the hall... Right opposite the entrance a dead man lay on the floor. He seemed to have succumbed to a heart attack... When we arrived the sentry squad was apparently already tired of tormenting people... Only now and then did they pull out one or the other who appeared to them suited as object of their sadistic pleasure... in groups we were driven in busses to the South Station in Frankfurt and there, all the while on the double, we had to run the gauntlet through a howling, stone-throwing crowd... We were put on an unheated special train there... and after the train was filled, it started moving into the night toward an unknown goal under the guard of the gendarmerie. On the way the order was given: "Remove your coats!"—so that we would be better exposed to the cold.... Soon we realized the direction, when, without stopping, we passed Erfurt and Eisenach at express-train speed. We were terrified, and the concentration camp of Weimar-Buchenwald, the most notorious of all, appeared before us...

We had not eaten anything for a long time now, and thirst was one of the worst torments that befell us, and this torment would stay with us until our release from the camp. First, all of our hair was cropped. When I looked around while this was being done, I

I would not wish to be a Jew in Germany.

—Hermann Göring, a top-ranking Nazi leader, November 12, 1938, right after *Kristallnacht*

discovered that at one spot of the square there was not one dead person, as in the Festhalle, but no less than four, lying one next to another... After hours of waiting, each one of us got a piece of fresh bread, and each group of ten men a container of so-called coffee. Each got a swallow, a mere drop for our parching thirst...

This report would never come to an end if I wanted to convey the many lesser and greater tortures to which we were subjected, for example, that as punishment for badly made beds we had to stand all night in front of the beds without sleep....

Many of the German Jews who escaped the Holocaust by emigrating left Germany during the very small window of time between November 1938 and the outbreak of war in September 1939. *Kristallnacht* convinced some foreign governments to ease their tight immigration restrictions for certain types of Jewish refugees. The British government agreed, for example, to allow some Jewish children under age seventeen to enter Great Britain from Germany and German-occupied territories, including Austria and the Czech lands. These *Kindertransporte* ("transports of children") saved the lives of a significant number of young Jewish boys and girls. But many of these children never saw their parents again. Olga Levy Ducker was put on a *Kindertransport* in 1939. In her 1992 memoir, Ducker describes the trip from Berlin to England.

This time there was no Papa to take care of passports. I was one of about a hundred children, from about four years old to seventeen. We were supervised by a few adults from the Jewish Refugee Committee, who carried our papers. German officers came strutting through our compartments. They checked us off on their lists. In their black uniforms; red, white, and black swastika armbands; high-peaked caps; and especially tall, polished boots, they looked menacing. One or two stopped to ask some of the children a question... As they passed me, one man looked at me and was about to speak. But his comrade pushed him from behind, pointing at his watch. They kept going.

With a shudder the train moved forward a few yards and stopped again... Now it was the turn of the Dutch customs officials. These men had smiles on their faces, and although we couldn't understand a word they said, we knew they were saying "Welcome to Holland." We all relaxed... Every now and then my fingers touched Oma's [grandma's] last-minute present, still stuffed into my pocket. Soon, I promised myself, I would open it.

Austrian Jewish children arrive in London as part of the Kinder-transport. These child transports saved several thousand young Jews before European borders closed at the start of the war. Most of these children never saw their parents again.

After a little while longer, we were allowed off the train. Down we spilled onto the platform, where the Dutch women were waiting for us. They gave us hot cocoa and cookies. They, too, had smiles on their faces.

But all too soon we were herded into a large room to wait for the ship. The Dutch harbor, Hoek van Holland, lies on the English Channel, directly across from a town in England called Harwich. The sea in the Channel is famous for its stormy winds and swelling waves. This night was typical.

With the cocoa and cookies swishing about in my stomach, I bravely boarded the ship. I was shown my cabin, which I was to share with another girl. She was older than I—maybe sixteen or seventeen. Up to now I had kept my feelings bottled up inside... But now, when I heard my cabin mate cry in her bed, I too began to feel a lump in my throat. I buried my head into my pillow, clenched my fists in fear and anger, and wept...

By daybreak we steamed into the harbor of Harwich. All was calm. Most of the people of that small fishing town were still asleep...But a few were there to greet us.

They spoke yet another language, which we did not understand.

I soon realized that my newly acquired phrase, "The dog is under the table," would be of no use to me in this situation. By chance, my fingers touched something in my pocket. It was Oma's present. I pulled out the little package and tore the paper off. Here were two tiny books, one blue, the other red. Each was so little, it could easily fit into the palm of my hand. These books were to prove my most valuable possessions in the next few months to come. They were dictionaries: one German to English, the other English to German.

In the beginning, these little friends were with me always. If I didn't understand what was being said to me which was most of the time—out would come my little red companion: English to German. I would simply hand it over to the speaker, who would show me the word. Then I would fish in my pocket for the blue one and find the reply in German. I would try to pronounce its English equivalent, which sometimes convulsed us both into laughter.

In April 1939, the German-owned Hamburg–America steamship line announced that the luxury liner *St. Louis* would soon leave on a special trip to Havana, Cuba. More than nine hundred Jews bought tickets, hoping that once they were in Cuba, they could wait in safety until their quota number came up in the United States. (Since the 1920s, only limited numbers, called a quota, of immigrants were allowed to enter the United States from each foreign country each year.) When the ship arrived at the Caribbean island, Cuban officials refused to let them get off the boat. The *St. Louis* was eventually forced to return to Europe. Max Korman was on board the *St. Louis.* His memoir describes the frustration and despair that began to spread among the passengers when they learned that they would not be allowed to enter Cuba.

Each of us became more and more tense and as our nerves began to fray we asked ourselves this question: with legal entry permits in hand, why had we journeyed for fourteen days across the ocean? to sit for three days in the port of Havana and to observe from a ship's railings the customs of the natives? One passenger, whose wife and two children were also on the ship, answered by slashing his wrists and jumping overboard. (A sailor leaped after him and saved his life.)...

In that mood we left the port, seeing Havana in all its glorious panorama: the dome of the capitol, the skyscrapers, the attractive landscaping, the palms.... The next morning, seemingly moving toward Cuba, we found ourselves looking at the coast of Florida: Miami's skyscrapers, beaches, the bridge to Key West. All these wonderful facilities seemed within a swimmer's reach. As the yachts and other luxury boats greeted us, you can well imagine the feeling

Jewish refugee Oskar Blechner stands with two other passengers on board the St. Louis. The ship eventually had to return to Europe, but Blechner survived the war in England. Other passengers given asylum in continental Europe were later murdered by the Nazis when the German army occupied the countries that had taken them in.

that dominated me. Here lived our uncle; this was the land to which I was supposed to come. And here I was so near, but oh so far.

. . . What rotten merchandise we must be if no one is prepared to accept us. The slaves must have been better: at least people paid for them, but here and now, when many wanted to pay for each of us, we are still rejected. Are we really so bad and so rotten? Are we really humanity's vermin and thus to be treated as lepers? . . .

To remind the world again of our fate, we decided to telegraph Roosevelt, the King of England (who was then visiting Washington), the American press and radio, and Jewish agencies in New York and Paris. We begged them to transfer us to another ship, which could be rented and which could await a favorable settlement of our fate . . .

Finally, on Saturday afternoon, as cables came to the *St. Louis* from European capitals and institutions, we realized that the critical stage of the negotiations had moved from the New World back to the Old World, from which we had come. Within thirty-six hours (we heard from Paris) we would have news of our fate . . . The thirty-six hours passed slowly, and with their passage the *St. Louis* came closer and closer to Hamburg, Germany, its home port. The thirty-sixth hour came and went without word from Paris. This we had expected. We were beyond despair.

The cable finally arrived: England, Holland, Belgium, and France had declared themselves ready to accept *us all* . . . We would land in Antwerp and from there be distributed to the host nations.

Shaping the Aryan Race

The project of a racial state also required the purification of the Aryan race itself. The Nazi plan to achieve this goal involved the forced sterilization of tens of thousands of Germans whom the Nazis believed were the carriers of dangerous genes. The Law for the Prevention of Genetically Diseased Offspring, decreed on July 14, 1933, and signed by Hitler, the minister of interior, and the minister of justice, listed the conditions that could require a person to be sterilized.

PAR. 1

1. Anyone who is suffering from a hereditary disease can be sterilized by a surgical operation if, according to the experiences of medical science, it is to be expected with great probability that his offspring will suffer from serious hereditary physical or mental defects.

Ernst G. Heppner was a German-Jew born in Breslau in 1921. His father and sister, who had stayed behind in Germany, were murdered in the Holocaust; a brother managed to flee to England. He describes his arrival in Shanghai, China, with his mother in February 1939.

So we were received by a committee, but we walked ashore then . . . again, no passport, no papers, nothing. And . . . there were many, many members of the Jewish community there looking for relatives perhaps that they expected. And we were loaded on trucks that normally carry pigs and moved to a reception center that had been furnished by one of the local residents where we were housed and received food.

2. Those who suffer from any of the following diseases are considered to be suffering from a hereditary disease within the meaning of this law:
(1) Mental deficiency from birth
(2) Schizophrenia
(3) Circular (manic-depressive) illness
(4) Hereditary epilepsy
(5) Hereditary St. Vitus' Dance...
(6) Hereditary blindness
(7) Hereditary deafness
(8) Serious hereditary physical deformation.
3. Furthermore, persons suffering severely from alcoholism can be sterilized.

PAR. 2

1. The person to be sterilized has the right to make an application...

PAR. 3

Sterilization can also be applied for by the following:
1. The civil service physician
2. For the inmates of a sanatorium, hospital, nursing home, or prison, by the head thereof.

PAR. 4

The application is to be made to the office of the Genetic Health Court....

PAR. 12

1. Once the Court has made its final decision for sterilization it must be carried out even against the will of the person to be sterilized. The civil service physician has to request the necessary measures from the police authorities. Where other measures are insufficient, direct force may be used.

The "biologically unworthy" were to be prevented from reproducing but healthy Aryan men and women were encouraged to produce as many children as possible. The Nazis believed that men and women had different, yet complementary natures, which were determined by their biology. Men were destined to be soldiers, statesmen, and workers. Women were supposed to produce and raise healthy Aryan children. In a speech given on September 8, 1934, to the National Socialist Women's Section of the Nazi party, Hitler insisted that "women's emancipation" was a Jewish lie, designed to weaken the Aryan race.

St. Vitus' Dance (Sydenham chorea)

A nervous disorder marked by spasmodic movements of the limbs and face

If the man's world is said to be the State, his struggle, his readiness to devote his powers to the service of the community, then it may perhaps be said that the woman's is a smaller world. For her world is her husband, her family, her children, and her home. But what would become of the greater world if there were no one to tend and care for the smaller one? How could the greater world survive if there were no one to make the cares of the smaller world the content of their lives?... The two worlds are not antagonistic. They complement each other, they belong together just as man and woman belong together...

The sacrifices which the man makes in the struggle of his nation, the woman makes in the preservation of that nation in individual cases. What the man gives in courage on the battlefield, the woman gives in eternal self-sacrifice, in eternal pain and suffering. Every child that a woman brings into the world is a battle, a battle waged for the existence of her people...

It is not true, as Jewish intellectuals assert, that respect depends on the overlapping of the spheres of activity of the sexes; this respect demands that neither sex should try to do that which belongs to the sphere of the other. It lies in the last resort in the fact that each knows that the other is doing everything necessary to maintain the whole community...

Whereas previously the programs of the liberal, intellectualist women's movements contained many points, the program of our National Socialist Women's movement has in reality but one single point, and that point is the child, that tiny creature which must be born and grow strong and which alone gives meaning to the whole life-struggle.

A Nazi poster praises a "healthy family, healthy children." Nazi propaganda promoted the importance of Aryan Germans marrying those with genetically "sound" family backgrounds.

Training Aryans for the Future

The Hitler Youth organization was one of the Nazis' most important instruments for indoctrinating the next generation of Aryan Germans in the values of the new racial community. Alfons Heck joined a Hitler Youth organization in 1938 at age ten. In his 1988 memoir he describes the effects the Hitler Youth activities had on the young recruits.

All these [physical] activities were designed to make us fit according to our motto: swift as greyhounds, tough as leather and hard as the steel of Krupp. In that, the Hitler Youth succeeded... Our prewar activities resembled those of the Boy Scouts, but with much more emphasis on discipline and political indoctrination.

Krupp

A major German armaments manufacturer

An ideal Aryan mother displays her eight children. For this service to the "racial community," she was awarded the Mother's Cross, which she wears around her neck. Women received a bronze cross for four children, silver for six, and gold for eight or more.

The paraphernalia, the parades, the flags and symbols, the soul-stirring music and the pomp and mysticism were very close in feeling to religious rituals. At the induction ceremony, my spine tingled in the conviction that I now belonged to something both majestic and threatened by bitter enemies. It was *Deutschland* [Germany]. . . . As the final act of the induction ceremony, we were handed the dagger with the Swastika inlaid in the handle and the inscription "Blood and Honor" on its blade. . . . I accepted the two basic tenets of the Nazi creed: belief in the innate superiority of the Germanic-Nordic race, and the conviction that total submission to Germany and to the *Führer* was our first duty.

Melita Maschmann became an important leader in the Nazi girls' youth organization. The publication of her memoir in Germany in the early 1960s represented one of the first attempts by a German woman to come to terms publicly with her involvement in the Nazi regime.

Whenever I probe the reasons which drew me to join the Hitler Youth, I always come up against this one: I wanted to escape from my childish, narrow life and I wanted to attach myself to something that was great and fundamental. This longing I shared with countless others of my contemporaries...

I believed the National Socialists when they promised to do away with unemployment and with it the poverty of six million people. I believed them when they said they would reunite the German nation, which had split into more than forty political parties, and overcome the consequences of the dictated peace of Versailles. And if my faith could only be based on hope in January 1933, it seemed soon enough to have deeds to point to.

...as my parents would not allow me to become a member of the Hitler Youth I joined secretly...I made up for what my new comrades had achieved before 1933, when it had cost personal sacrifices to belong to the National Socialist Youth. But...what now awaited me was a bitter disappointment, the extent of which I dared not admit to myself. The evening meetings for which we met in a dark and grimy cellar were fatally lacking in interest.

The time was passed in paying subscriptions, drawing up countless lists and swotting up [learning] the words of songs, the linguistic poverty of which I was unable to ignore, although I made a great effort to do so. Discussions on political texts from, say, *Mein Kampf* quickly ended in general silence...I remember with more pleasure the weekend outings, with hikes, sports, campfires and youth hostelling. Occasionally there would be "field exercises" with neighbouring groups. If there was any rivalry between them the game often degenerated into a first class brawl. What kind of a picture these girls fighting over a flag would have presented to an outsider I prefer not to imagine.

But for me, not even the outings made up for the tedium of the remaining "duties." In my group I was the only girl attending a secondary school. The others were shop girls, office workers, dressmakers and servant girls. So my desire to be accepted into the community of "working youth" had been fulfilled. The fact that this fulfilment was a bitter disappointment I explained to myself thus: these girls came from the lower middle class and regarded the "wellborn daughters" I was trying to escape from with envy...

My secret entry into the Hitler Youth dated from March 1, 1933, and all the leading positions were occupied by the so called "Old Guard."...They were sometimes painfully coarse and primitive...It was then that I first consciously said to myself: Party leaders can make mistakes like everyone else; perhaps there are also rogues and charlatans amongst them who have wormed their way into office because they are hungry for power...If they

A typical Hitler Youth poster encourages boys to join the organization: "Youth serves the Führer—All ten-year-olds should go into the Hitler Youth." Hitler Youth membership became obligatory for boys in 1936.

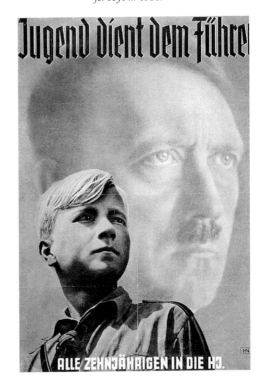

dream up such shameless lies, the people who are not well enough educated to be able to judge for themselves will fall for their nonsense. Anyone who observes this should not be silent about it. But one also has no right to turn one's back on the Party on account of such disillusionments. Gradually the spirit of truth will prevail over the lies...I always returned to the hope that within a few generations we should succeed in educating every German to be a decent National Socialist. I wanted to share in the task of this educational work. For this reason I stayed in the Hitler Youth. I wanted to help create the *Volksgemeinschaft* [racial community] in which people would live together as in one big family.

The indoctrination of young Germans did not take place only in the Hitler Youth. Nazi ideology also permeated the regular school curriculum, as these test questions in mathematics textbooks demonstrate.

Question 95: The construction of a lunatic asylum costs 6 million RM [Reichsmarks]. How many houses at 15,000 RM each could have been built for that amount?

Question 97: To keep a mentally ill person costs approx. 4 RM per day, a cripple 5.50 RM, a criminal 3.50 RM. Many civil servants receive only 4 RM per day, white collar employees barely 3.50 RM, unskilled workers not even 2 RM per head for their fami-

A teacher gives her class the Hitler salute. Her students have learned early in life to return this Hitler greeting.

lies,...Illustrate these figures with a diagram. —According to conservative estimates, there are 300,000 mentally ill, epileptics etc, in care...How much do these people cost to keep in total, at a cost of 4 RM per head?...How many marriage loans at 1000 RM each...could be granted from this money?

...A modern night bomber can carry 1,800 incendiaries. How long (in kilometres) is the path along which it can distribute these bombs if it drops a bomb every second at a speed of 250 km per hour? How far apart are the craters from one another...? How many kilometres can 10 such planes set alight if they fly 50 metres apart from one another? How many fires are caused if 1/3 of the bombs hit their targets and of these 1/3 ignite?

The SS and the Concentration Camp System

For those who could not fit, or did not want to fit into Hitler's new racial state there were the concentration camps. Heinrich Himmler made the concentration camp system into the foundation of an SS empire by tirelessly persecuting and incarcerating an ever growing list of Nazi Germany's racial, biological, and political enemies including Socialists and Communists, Jews, Gypsies, Jehovah's Witnesses, gay men, prostitutes, the homeless, beggars, and other "antisocial elements." Himmler constructed a terrifying police state consisting of the Gestapo, the SD (*Sicherheitsdienst,* meaning "security service," originally the internal party security force), and concentration camps into which tens of thousands of victims were thrown and from which many never emerged alive. In a speech given to army soldiers in January 1937, Himmler explained the role of concentration camps.

It would be extremely instructive for everyone...to inspect such a concentration camp. Once they have seen it, they are convinced of the fact that no one had been sent there unjustly; that it is the offal [garbage] of criminals and freaks. No better demonstration of the laws of inheritance and race...exists than such a concentration camp. There you can find people with hydrocephalus, people who are cross-eyed, deformed, half-Jewish, and a number of racially inferior subjects. All that is assembled there. Of course we distinguish between those inmates who are only there for a few months for the purpose of education, and those who are to stay for a very long time. On the whole, education

Marriage Loans

To encourage "racially valuable" German couples to marry and have children, the Nazis introduced marriage loans to help newlyweds acquire the basic items they needed to set up a new household. In 1939, 42 percent of all couples who married received a marriage loan. But there is little evidence that the marriage loan scheme significantly raised the marriage rate or the birth rate.

hydrocephalus

A condition in which fluid accumulates in the brain cavity resulting in atrophy of the brain

consists of discipline, never of any kind of instruction on an ideological basis, for the prisoners have, for the most part, slave-like souls; and only very few people of real character can be found there... The discipline thus squeezes order out of them. The order begins with these people living in clean barracks. Such a thing can really only be accomplished by us Germans; hardly another nation would be as humane as we are.... The people are taught to wash themselves twice daily, and to use a toothbrush with which most of them have been unfamiliar... It is... necessary to keep the number of such guards for concentration camps—there are 3,500 men currently in Germany—at a relatively high level, for no form of service is as exacting and strenuous for troops as the guarding of crooks and criminals..

In case of war, it must become clear to us that a considerable number of unreliable persons will have to be put here if we are to

A 1945 map of Germany shows the prisons, concentration camps, and work camps that spread across the German landscape after the Nazis came to power.

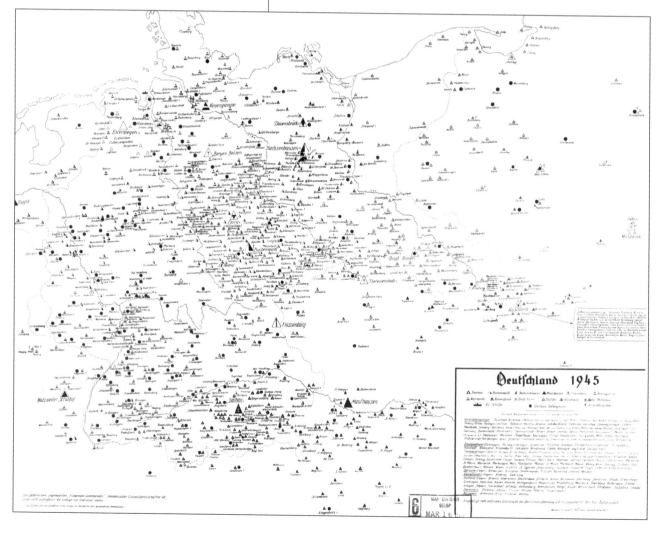

assure ourselves of the absence of highly disagreeable developments in case of war.

The prisoner guards were formerly members of the general SS. We gradually collected them into the so-called Death's Head Units... In such camps there are two or three control towers, manned day and night with fully loaded machine guns, so that any attempt at a general uprising—a possibility for which we must always be prepared—can be immediately suppressed. The entire camp can be strafed from three towers...

We must clearly recognize that an opponent in war is an opponent not only in a military but also in an ideological sense. When I speak here of opponents, I obviously mean our natural opponent, international Bolshevism [communism]... This Bolshevism, of course, has its supreme citadel in Russia. But this does not mean that there is danger of Bolshevist attack from Russia only. One must always reckon with this danger from wherever this Jewish Bolshevism has gained decisive influence for itself...

Let us all clearly realize that the next decades... signify a fight of extermination of the above-mentioned subhuman opponents in the whole world who fight Germany, as the nuclear people of the Northern race; Germany, as nucleus of the German people; Germany, as bearer of the culture of mankind. They signify the existence or nonexistence of the white race of which we are the leading people.

Lina Haag and her husband were members of the German Communist Party who were arrested by the Nazis in 1933. She was sent to a series of prisons and then, finally, to the Lichtenberg concentration camp for women. In 1947, she published a memoir describing her experiences.

We are lined up in one of the courtyards. About thirty women: political prisoners, Jews, criminals, prostitutes, and Jehovah's Witnesses. Female guards from the SS circle us like gray wolves. I see this new ideal type of German woman for the first time. Some have blank faces and some have brutal looks, but they all have the same mean expression around their mouths. They pace back and forth with long strides and fluttering gray capes, their commanding voices ring shrilly across the court, and the large wolfhounds with them strain threateningly at their leashes...

I always thought that after two years of solitary confinement nothing more in this world could frighten me, but I was wrong. I am terribly afraid of the beatings, of the dark cells in which

Concentration Camp Badges

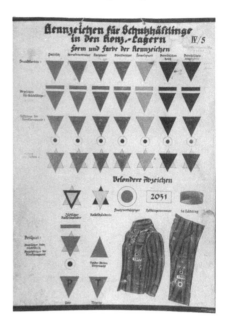

The badges that inmates were forced to wear made it easy for the SS guards, and also for the other inmates, to see where a particular person fit into the (increasingly racial) hierarchy of the concentration camps. For example, criminals wore green inverted triangles, political prisoners wore red ones, "asocials" (a broad category including gypsies, homeless people, and prostitutes) wore black triangles. Gay men were identified by pink triangles and Jehovah's Witnesses (persecuted because their religion prevented them from serving in the army or taking an oath to Hitler) by purple ones. Jews wore the yellow Jewish star. How high a prisoner stood in the camp hierarchy might mean the difference between life and death. In the absurd racial worldview of the SS, serious criminals, such as murderers, who were nonetheless "racially German" ranked higher than Jews or Gypsies. Aryan criminals were given positions of responsibility in the camps as the bosses of other inmates.

An aerial view of Dachau concentration camp taken during the war shows how large this installation had become. The Nazis increased the numbers of orderly rows of barracks to accommodate the ever-expanding number of their real and imagined political and racial enemies.

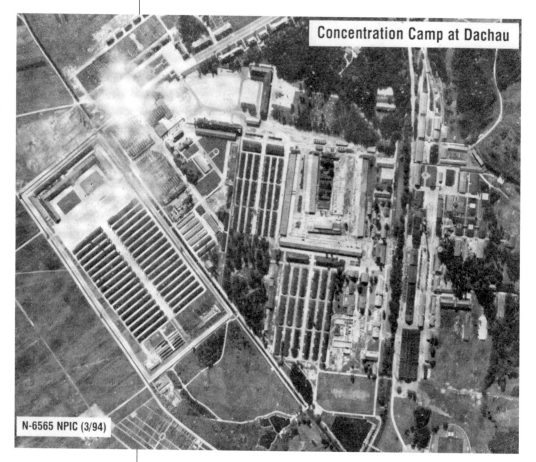

Concentration Camp at Dachau

N-6565 NPIC (3/94)

women die so quickly, and of the dreaded chambers in which prisoners are interrogated by Gestapo officials... What cannot be found in this hellish place! Fear is torment enough; torment enough is the certainty that these things will happen to us one day. It is absolutely impossible to be here for years without disaster striking one day... One day it will come. Either through the denunciation of a "comrade," or because of the guard, or because a shoe string was not properly tied, or because the work wasn't adequate, or because of fishing a potato or bread crust out of the pigsty... Anyone who gets out of here is granted the gift of life...

Not that we have no laws here. These are the moods of the camp commandant, the orders that he shouts across the prison yard. He has the revolver and the power over life and death. When he screams, everyone has to scramble, even the guards and all the she-wolves too, the dogs and us. When he strides across the courtyard, when he marches by the lines of fear and misery, hundreds of pairs of hate-filled eyes stare after him. A veritable cloud of hate envelops him. It almost seems to me as if he needs this hate as much as the air he breathes...

It is incomprehensible to us that there are so many sadists. Are they really sadists, criminals by nature, murderers? I don't think so... They are just respectable petty bourgeois conformists. Only they happen to be employed not in the tax office, but in the police office. They happen not to be municipal clerks, or meat packers, or office assistants, or construction workers, or accountants, but are instead Gestapo employees and SS men. They do not distinguish between good and evil; they simply do what they are ordered to do. They are not ordered to distinguish between good and evil, or between right and wrong, but to rid the state of enemies and destroy them. They do this with the same stubborn pedantry, the same German industriousness, and the same German thoroughness with which they would otherwise check tax returns or write minutes or butcher pigs. They whip a defenseless woman tied to a post with matter-of-fact earnestness and conscientiousness, fully convinced that in so doing they are serving the state or their Führer, which is the same to them... They are not born sadists, nor professional criminals, nor impassioned murderers, but just small-minded middle-class conformists. Like everyone else. The same talent for organization that works on the outside to improve the people's physical fitness with goose-stepping and vitamin drops drives the mortality rates here in the concentration camps ever higher.

If a prisoner attempts to escape, he is to be shot without warning.... If a unit of prisoners mutinies or revolts, it is to be shot at by all supervising guards. Warning shots are forbidden on principle.
—SS Service Regulations for Prisoner Escorts and Guards, 1933

Frightened prisoners line up in Sachsenhausen concentration camp, north of Berlin, in 1938. The Nazis built Sachsenhausen as a model for other concentration camps. Here they trained such men as Rudolf Höss, commandant of the notorious Nazi death camp Auschwitz.

Chapter Five

Hitler's War

After he came to power, Hitler tore up the Versailles Treaty and made it clear to the world that the Third Reich had no intention of remaining a second-rate power. In 1935, he reintroduced universal military service to build up a new, large conscript army. In 1936, he sent troops into the Rhineland, even though this western border region was to remain a demilitarized zone, according to the settlement reached following World War I. In 1938, Hitler annexed Austria. The British and the French did nothing. Haunted by memories of the carnage of the First World War, they were not willing to risk a second. To avoid war, the British and the French were even prepared to make Czechoslovakia give Hitler the western border zone called the Sudetenland when he claimed in 1938 that the Czechs were oppressing ethnic Germans who lived there. In the spring of 1939, Hitler's new army occupied the rest of Czechoslovakia. This was Hitler's last bloodless victory.

Germans were impressed by Hitler's foreign policy successes. But, like the British and the French, they, too, were terrified by the idea of repeating World War I. In Poland, Hitler's army showed, however, that there was an alternative to the enormously destructive and futile trench warfare of 1914 to 1918. Hitler's new type of highly mobile, mechanized "lightning warfare" (blitzkrieg) defeated Poland in a matter of weeks. Leading the assault, Hitler's modern airforce (luftwaffe) attacked Polish planes while they were still on the ground, crippled communications, and bombed troop formations and civilian targets, such as the capital city of Warsaw. Armored divisions of tanks (Panzers) led the ground attack, providing a moving shield of steel behind which motorized infantry in trucks could follow and secure the areas overrun by the tanks. This new formula gave the Germans quick, cheap victories. The Nazis attacked Poland on September 4, 1939, and were able to declare victory on October 6. Some 200,000 Poles were reported as killed, wounded, or missing and the Germans took 900,000 prisoners but German casualties were just 45,000 killed, wounded, or missing.

A woman in the Sudetenland, the western border region of Czechoslovakia, weeps while she gives the Hitler salute to the German troops marching into her country in 1938. British and French leaders hoped that giving Hitler this ethnic German region would ensure peace. Instead, Hitler saw this concession as a sign of weakness, and in spring of 1939 he invaded the rest of Czechoslovakia.

The campaign against France in the spring and summer of 1940 was the real test of blitzkrieg. It passed with flying colors. After successfully invading Denmark and Norway in April, Hitler's army (Wehrmacht) turned west against France, Britain, Holland, and Belgium in May of 1940. The Western Allies had more tanks and men but the Germans were more experienced in the new type of lightning warfare. By the end of June 1940, the German armies had overrun northern France and the French were forced to sign a humiliating armistice. The British Army, though escaping across the Channel back to England with 338,000 men, was forced to abandon virtually all of its equipment on the beaches of Dunkirk, France. The Germans were ecstatic. In less than two months, Hitler had achieved what the imperial kaiser's army had never managed despite more than four years of bitter, costly trench warfare—the defeat and humiliation of France and the occupation of Paris.

Yet, Britain was still in the war. In July 1940, Hitler gave the order to prepare an invasion, Operation Sea Lion. Yet, he was not prepared to risk his ships, men, and military equipment in a treacherous crossing of the English Channel, which separates Britain from France, without first gaining air superiority. Hitler therefore gave the order to Hermann Goering, chief of the German

A map of German military action between 1939 and 1942 illustrates the success of Hitler's Blitzkrieg in the early years of the war. However, success quickly turned to failure as German military power was fatally overextended in the invasion of the Soviet Union in the summer of 1941.

GERMAN MILITARY OFFENSIVES, 1939–1942

→ German Advances   - - - Extent of German Advances

Luftwaffe, to destroy Britain's air power by bombing Royal Air Force (RAF) airfields in the south of England as well as British war industries. In September 1940, German air raids began to target London and other British cities. This German air offensive killed forty thousand civilians but it also took the lives of some two thousand German airmen. The Germans lost more than 2,200 aircraft. Hitler's air force was unable to destroy British air defenses so that a German cross-Channel invasion of the British Isles had to be put on hold indefinitely. Hitler then turned to the Soviet Union.

Racial War and War of Plunder

The German war against Poland quickly revealed the brutal racism of the Nazi regime. In a memorandum to Hitler dated May 25, 1940, Heinrich Himmler explained what the Nazi racial empire in the East would mean for the subject peoples.

For the non-German population of the East there must be no higher school than the four-grade elementary school. The sole goal of this school is to be simple arithmetic—[being able to count] up to five hundred at the most; writing of one's name; the doctrine that it is a divine law to obey the Germans and to be honest, industrious, and good. I don't think that reading is necessary. Apart from this school there are to be no schools at all in the East. . . .

The population will, as a people of laborers without leaders, be at our disposal and will furnish Germany annually with migrant workers and with workers for special tasks (roads, quarries, buildings) . . . They will, under the strict, consistent, and just leadership of the German people, be called upon to help work on its everlasting cultural tasks and its buildings and perhaps, as far as the amount of heavy work is concerned, will be the ones who make the realization of these tasks possible.

In Western Europe, the occupying German forces presented a quite different face. In France, the Germans were even prepared to "collaborate" with a new French government set up in the southern unoccupied zone in the resort town of Vichy under the leadership of the First World War military leader and national hero Marshal Petain. Still, the Nazis did force the French to deliver massive amounts of food and war matériel. A report published after the war listed the percentages of annual industrial and agricultural production that France was required to deliver to Germany.

The Stuka dive bombers were an essential element of the new Blitzkrieg. To make these attacks even more frightening, the Stukas were equipped with air-activated sirens that emitted a shrill sound as the plane dropped down on its target.

Divided and Conquered

The General Government was one of two parts of the western half of Poland that the Germans conquered and occupied between 1939 and 1941 under the terms of their non-aggression agreement with the Soviet Union. The General Government was ruled directly by the Germans but not annexed into the Reich. The westernmost region, the *Warthegau*, on Germany's eastern border, was incorporated directly into the new expanded Germany.

Coal, 29 per cent; electric power, 22 per cent; petroleum and motor fuel, 80 per cent; iron ore, 74 per cent; steel products, crude and half-finished, 51 per cent; copper, 75 per cent; lead, 43 per cent; zinc, 38 per cent; tin, 67 per cent; nickel 64 per cent; mercury, 50 per cent; platinum, 76 per cent; bauxite, 40 per cent; aluminium, 75 per cent; magnesium, 100 per cent; sulphur carbonate, 80 per cent; industrial soap, 67 per cent; vegetable oil, 40 per cent; carbosol [a chemical used for degreasing and cleaning], 100 per cent; rubber, 38 per cent; paper and cardboard, 16 per cent; wool, 59 per cent; cotton, 53 per cent; flax, 65 per cent; leather 67 per cent; cement 55 per cent; lime, 20 per cent; acetone, 21 per cent.

Levies of manufactured goods and the products of the mining industry:
Automobile construction, 70 per cent; electrical and radio construction, 45 per cent; industrial precision parts, 100 per cent; heavy castings, 100 per cent; foundries, 46 per cent; chemical industries, 34 per cent; rubber industry, 60 per cent; paint and varnish, 60 per cent; perfume, 33 per cent; wool industry, 28 per cent; cotton weaving, 15 per cent; flax and cotton weaving, 12 per cent; industrial hides, 20 per cent; buildings and public works, 75 per cent; wood work and furniture, 50 per cent; lime and cement, 68 per cent; naval construction, 79 per cent; aeronautic construction, 90 per cent.

The Battle of Britain

By the summer of 1940, Hitler's only unconquered opponent was Britain. He hoped to pave the way for an attack by weakening British air power. A British illustrated chronicle of the Battle of Britain published in 1940 offered its explanation of why Hermann Goering's bombing strategy failed.

The air offensive against Britain started in full force on 8 August. From then until the 19th when there was a temporary lull, bombers came over almost continuously, attacking aerodromes, dockyards, and munition works. High explosive and incendiary bombs were released over military and non-military objectives, but the damage done by the raiders, hopelessly outclassed by the British fighters and harried by a death-dealing barrage of anti-aircraft fire, was out of all proportion to the losses they suffered... The phenomenal successes of the British fighter pilots in their combats with the Nazi raiders were due in large measure to

A German poster tells French citizens to trust German soldiers. It presents a picture of a smiling German caring for children "abandoned" by their parents in the rush to escape the invading German armies.

their unbounded faith in their machines. Both the "Hurricane" and the "Spitfire" fighters proved themselves time and time again to be faster and more manoeuvrable than their German counterparts, besides possessing a more powerful and more devastating armament in their eight machine guns. In spite of their best efforts the Messerschmidts escorting the German bombers failed to keep their more nimble opponents at bay or to prevent them from taking a terrible toll of their bomber formations... The accumulation of scrap material from planes shot down in Britain became almost embarrassing to the authorities, and a central dump ... was established where the useful material was sorted out for conversion in due course into new British planes.

Hitler examines a battle map with his generals at a planning session in 1940. Hitler insisted on taking complete control of military strategy and claiming the credit for the German army's successes.

Goering argued that air raids on population centers would disrupt British war industry and destroy the British will to fight. The attacks on London and other British cities did neither. The American journalist Edward R. Murrow, who was stationed in London, described the reaction of Londoners to the German air attacks in a radio broadcast on September 10, 1940.

We are told today that the Germans believe that Londoners... will rise up and demand a new government, one that will make peace with Germany. It's more probable that they'll rise up and murder a few German pilots who come down by parachute...

The politicians who called this a "people's war" were right... I've seen some horrible sights in this city during these days and nights, but not once have I heard man, woman or child suggest that Britain should throw in her hand. These people are angry. How much they can stand, I don't know. The strain is very great... After four days and nights of this air blitzkrieg, I think the people here are rapidly becoming veterans...

Many people have already got over the panicky feeling that hit everyone in the nerve centers when they realized they were being bombed. Those people I talked to in long queues in front of the big

London civilians spend the night in the Elephant & Castle underground train station during a German bombing raid on the British capital in November 1940. Between 1939 and 1945, about 40,000 British civilians were killed by German air raids.

public shelters tonight were cheerful and somewhat resigned. They'd been waiting in line for an hour or more, waiting for the shelters to open at the first wail of the sirens... they carried blankets to throw over the chairs in this public underground shelter...

Of course, they don't like the situation, but most of them feel that even this underground existence is preferable to what they'd get under German domination.

The Invasion of the Soviet Union

Frustrated with his failure to knock Britain out of the war before he turned against the Soviet Union, Hitler was nonetheless impatient to begin his great "crusade" against Nazism's major ideological enemy, Russian Communism. He also needed the Soviet Union's enormous resources to continue fighting against Britain. In the longer view, Hitler envisioned a vast new empire in the East that would make

Germany a dominant world power. Hitler described his plans for the occupied eastern territories to his inner circle during late 1941 and early 1942 at his East Prussian headquarters. Hitler's remarks were recorded by a member of his entourage.

The essential thing, for the moment, is to conquer... Our role in Russia will be analogous to that of England in India... The Russian space is our India. Like the English, we shall rule this empire with a handful of men. It would be a mistake to claim to educate the native. All that we could give him would be a half-knowledge— just what's needed to conduct a revolution!...

Our guiding principle must be that these people have but one justification for existence—to be of use to us economically. We must concentrate on extracting from these territories everything that it is possible to extract. As an incentive to them to deliver their agricultural produce to us, and to work in our mines and armament factories, we will open shops all over the country at which they will be able to purchase such manufactured articles as they want... In the field of public health there is no need whatsoever to extend to the subject races the benefits of our own knowledge. This would result only in an enormous increase in local populations, and I absolutely forbid the organisation of any sort of hygiene or cleanliness crusades in these territories. Compulsory vaccination will be confined to Germans alone, and the doctors in the German colonies will be there solely for the purpose of looking after the German colonists. It is stupid to thrust happiness upon people against their wishes. Dentistry, too, should remain a closed book to them...

The most foolish mistake we could possibly make would be to allow the subject races to possess arms. History shows that all conquerors who have allowed their subject races to carry arms have prepared their own downfall by so doing... So let's not have any native militia or police. German troops alone will bear the sole responsibility for the maintenance of law and order throughout the occupied Russian territories, and a system of military strong-points must be evolved to cover the entire occupied country.

A German tank moves deeper into the Soviet Union in October 1941. Hitler's Blitzkrieg (lightning war) used tanks, planes, and infantry in motorized units in coordinated and rapid strikes that quickly defeated Poland and France.

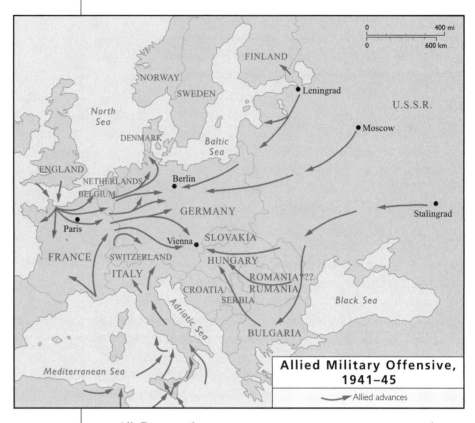

Allied Military Offensive, 1941–45

→ Allied advances

All Germans living in territories must remain in personal contact with these strong-points. The whole must be most carefully organised to conform with the long-term policy of German colonisation, and our colonising penetration must be constantly progressive, until it reaches the stage where our own colonists far outnumber the local inhabitants.

The Nazis viewed people of Slavic ethnicity, including Poles and Russians, as inferior. Hitler's brutal, racist plan for occupying the Soviet Union was supported by some of his top military commanders as well as by many ordinary German soldiers. In October 1941, for example, Field Marshal Walther von Reichenau issued the following order to his troops.

The most essential aim of war against the Jewish-Bolshevistic [the Nazis believed communism was a Jewish idea and that the Soviet Union was run by Jews.] system is a complete destruction of their means of power and the elimination of Asiatic influence from the European culture. In this connection the troops are facing tasks which exceed the one-sided routine of soldiering. The soldier in the eastern territories is not merely a fighter according to the rules of the art of war but also a bearer of ruthless national ideology and the avenger of bestialities which have been inflicted upon German and racially related nations...

The combatting of the enemy behind the front line is still not being taken seriously enough. Treacherous, cruel partisans [irregular fighters operating behind German lines] are still being made prisoners of war and guerilla fighters dressed partly in uniforms or plain clothes and vagabonds are still being treated as proper soldiers, and sent to prisoner-of-war camps...The feeding of the natives and of prisoners of war who are not working for the Armed Forces from Army kitchens is an equally misunderstood humanitarian act as is the giving of cigarettes and bread...When retreating, the Soviets have often set buildings on fire. The troops should be interested in extinguishing of fires only as far as it is necessary to secure sufficient numbers of billets. Otherwise the disappearance of symbols of the former bolshevistic rule even in the form of buildings is part of the struggle of destruction. Neither historic nor artistic considerations are of any importance in the eastern territories.

Karl X. was a member of the SS who had served in France and was then sent to Russia where he was killed in action in 1943. He wrote a letter home in the fall of 1941.

The East, September 9th, '41

My Dear Ones,

After a long delay, I am finally able to write you again...It was a joyful trip from Wednesday to Sunday. To me it felt like a holiday, the trip went like a fever chart, from the capital to the cornfields of Prussia, from there up once more to the capital of Litauen [Lithuania] and then southeast, to the capital of White Russia, which is now German territory. A beautiful environment, in the middle of woods in a former tank camp. But the roads over here—well I can't describe them, but the field paths back home are made of gold by comparison. I saw one good road, and drove on it for a while, a motorway, the only one in the Soviet Union from Minsk to Moscow. And then the Russian economy—I have had a peek into a few of the houses. I can only say, I would feel better in one of our chicken coops. Up to now it is a good-natured group here, three of us sleep

German soldiers advance into Russia in 1941; the soldier on the right is about to throw a granade. To crush the Soviet Union, Hitler assembled a massive force of 3.2 million German troops. Germany's allies contributed about 800,000 additional men. By 1945, millions of Germans had been killed or wounded on this bloody Eastern Front or had disappeared into Soviet prisoner-of-war camps.

German soldiers photograph two Soviet citizens executed by the Germans for alleged partisan activity, such as sabotaging German supplies. Germans committed a great number of atrocities and war crimes in the Soviet Union.

together in one room. We have closets and a bed, a furnace, even electric lights. And, lastly, I want to congratulate father on his birthday. I couldn't do it before, because it was not decided yet if we could keep our old field post numbers.

And now for today, best wishes from Karl

Warm greetings to little Hans.

The German military authorities in the East were not particularly concerned about the fate of the millions of Soviet prisoners of war (POWs) captured as the German Army rolled toward Moscow. Between June 1941 and February 1942 alone, some two million captured Russian soldiers died of starvation, disease, and mistreatment in German POW camps in Poland or concentration camps in Germany. An unidentified eyewitness described conditions in a prisoners' camp in Poland. This testimony was published in a 1946 Polish report on German crimes in Poland.

The camp consists of four huts, situated in the fields near the village, so that everything that happens there can be observed by the neighbours. Train-loads of prisoners which arrived here had taken over a fortnight to reach the new camp and were without food or water. Each wagon when opened contained scores of dead bodies. The sick who could not move were thrown out. They were ordered to sit down on the ground near the camp and were shot by the S.S.-men before the eyes of the rest. The camp contains about 2,500 prisoners. The average daily death-rate is about 50. The dead bodies are thrown out on to the fields and sprinkled with lime, often lying some days after that unburied.... The prisoners received 1/4 kg of bread made of horse-chestnut flour and potato-skins, and soup made of rotten cabbage.

The End of Blitzkrieg

During the first few weeks of the Russian campaign, the Germans made incredible gains. By the end of July 1941, the Wehrmacht had captured more than one million prisoners, occupied thousands of square miles of territory, and destroyed 1,500 Soviet tanks. Yet the Germans were not able to annihilate the Soviet Army and achieve a decisive victory. In a diary entry written in August, the German general Franz Halder explained why.

The whole situation makes it increasingly plain that we have underestimated the Russian colossus, who consistently prepared for war with that utterly ruthless determination so characteristic of totalitarian States... At the outset of the war we reckoned with about 200 enemy divisions. Now we have already counted 360. These divisions indeed are not armed and equipped according to our standards, and their tactical leadership is often poor. But there they are, and if we smash a dozen of them, the Russians simply put up another dozen. The time factor favors them, as they are near their own resources, whereas we are moving farther and farther away from ours. And so our troops, sprawled over an immense front line, without any depth, are subjected to the enemy's incessant attacks. Sometimes these are successful, because in these enormous spaces too many gaps have to be left open.

The deeper the Germans went into Russia, the greater their problems of supply and reinforcement. Soon, the weather also became an enemy. On December 5, 1941, as German front-line soldiers advanced into the northern Moscow suburbs, the Russians launched a massive counteroffensive. Two days later, the commander-in-chief of Army Group Center (there were two other Army Groups: North and South), Fedor von Bock made a report that summarized the obstacles facing the German Army.

Invading German soldiers in white winter uniforms move through a snow-laden Russian forest. German soldiers discovered that the bitter Russian winter could be as deadly an enemy as the Soviet Army.

The anxiety of the German people about the Eastern Front is increasing. Deaths owing to freezing are an especially important factor in this connection. The number of cases of freezing revealed by transports from the Eastern Front back home is so enormous as to cause great indignation here and there.... Soldiers' mail, too, has a devastating effect. Words cannot describe what our soldiers are writing back home from the front.

—Joseph Goebbels, Hitler's propaganda minister, in his diary, January 22, 1942

Three things have led to the present crisis:

1. The setting in of the autumn mud season. Troop movements and supplies were almost completely paralyzed by the mud-covered road...
2. The failure of the railways.
   Weaknesses in the organization, a shortage of wagons, of locomotives and of trained personnel—the inability of the locomotives and the equipment to withstand the Russian winter.
3. The underestimation of the enemy's resistance and of his reserves of men and material.

The Russians have understood how to increase our transport difficulties by destroying almost all the bridges on the main lines and roads to such an extent that the front lacks the basic necessities of life and of fighting equipment. Ammunition, fuel, food, and winter clothing do not reach the front line...

The Russians have managed in a surprisingly short time to reconstitute divisions which have been smashed, to bring new ones from Siberia, Iran, and the Caucasus up to the threatened front, and to replace the artillery which has been lost by numerous rocket launchers... By contrast, the strength of the German divisions has sunk to less than half as a result of the unbroken fighting and of the winter, which has arrived with full force; the fighting strength of the tanks is even less.

The Tide Turns

On December 8, 1941, the United States declared war on Japan, a day after the Japanese had launched a surprise air and submarine attack on the U.S. Navy in its main Pacific base at Pearl Harbor, Hawaii. Hitler already had made an alliance with Japan but this agreement did not require him to join the Japanese in their war against America. Nevertheless, on December 11, Hitler declared war on the United States. In an official statement, the Nazis blamed the U.S. government for provoking the war.

The Government of the United States having violated in the most flagrant manner and in ever-increasing measure all rules of neutrality in favor of the adversaries of Germany and having continually been guilty of the most severe provocations toward Germany ever since the outbreak of the European war, provoked by the British declaration of war against Germany on September 3, 1939, has finally resorted to open military acts of aggression.

On September 11, 1941, the President of the United States publicly declared that he had ordered the American Navy and Air Force to shoot on sight at any German war vessel. In his speech of October 27, 1941, he once more expressly affirmed that this order was in force. Acting under this order, vessels of the American Navy, since early September 1941, have systematically attacked German naval forces. Thus, American destroyers...have opened fire on German submarines according to plan. The Secretary of the American Navy, Mr. Knox, himself confirmed that American destroyers attacked German submarines...Although Germany on her part has strictly adhered to the rules of international law in her relations with the United States during every period of the present war, the Government of the United States from initial violations of neutrality has finally proceeded to open acts of war against Germany. The Government of the United States has thereby virtually created a state of war.

A solemn Hitler announces the German declaration of war against the United States to the German Parliament on December 11, 1941. U.S. entry into the European war, combined with Hitler's failure to defeat the Soviet Union, eventually led to the utter defeat of Nazi Germany.

Hitler hoped that the Japanese would keep the United States occupied in the Pacific until he had defeated the Soviet Union. Direct U.S. military participation in the European war was indeed limited for some time to come. Nevertheless, American involvement in the European conflict was vital. America sent large amounts of military equipment to both Britain and the Soviet Union. And with the joint U.S and British invasion of North Africa in November 1942, the Americans also began to participate in a series of military campaigns against the Nazis. These campaigns moved from North Africa to Italy, opening up a Southern Front that drained off significant German supplies of men and matériel. In a speech delivered in Berlin on September 10, 1943, Hitler insisted that Italy's recent surrender to the Allies would have no important effect on Germany's ability to win the war.

The collapse of Italy...was not really due to Italy's inability to defend herself adequately or to the fact that the necessary German help was not forthcoming. Rather it was due to those Italians who caused the capitulation by their systematic sabotage... The Italian leaders have deserted their ally, the German Reich, and gone over to our common enemy.

We have just begun to fight!

PEARL HARBOR
BATAAN
CORAL SEA
MIDWAY
GUADALCANAL
NEW GUINEA
BISMARCK SEA
CASABLANCA
ALGIERS
TUNISIA

An American war poster lists all of the places that American troops are fighting by 1942. The last three sites are in North Africa. Although American military efforts were at this time concentrated in the Pacific against the Japanese, the United States had begun to make an important contribution to the fight against Hitler.

...Italy's withdrawal [from the war]means little in a military sense because in reality the struggle in that country has really been carried on for months mainly by German forces.

Now we can continue the struggle freed of all encumbrances... I believe unconditionally in success, a belief grounded in my own life and in the destiny of our people.

In 1939 we were alone and isolated when we had to face the declarations of war. We acted in the belief that teaches us that heroic resistance is much better than any cowardly submission. I declared as early as September 1, 1939, in my speech to the Reichstag that the German people would be brought to their knees by neither time nor force of arms...

We expect in just these times that the nation will fulfill its duty defiantly and with dogged determination in all spheres. It has every reason to have confidence in itself. The home front can look with pride upon its soldiers, who, with heroic sacrifice of their blood, perform their duties under the most difficult circumstances. The men at the front, too, who have endured under superhuman burdens through many weeks and months, must also remember the homeland, which today has also become a fighting front. Here old men, boys, mothers, women, and girls do their duty...

Our future generations will one day express their gratitude in the knowledge that here a free and socially secure life has been won through the greatest sacrifice. I take pride that I am the leader of this nation and I am grateful to God for every hour he grants me so that through my work I can win the greatest struggle of our times.

The measures we have taken for the protection of German interests in Italy are very hard indeed. Insofar as they affect Italy, they are being applied according to a preconceived plan and the results already have been good.

...The fate of Italy is a lesson to us never, in the hour of gravest crisis and deep distress, to forsake the commandment of national honor but to stand steadfastly by our allies, and to do what duty commands.

To a people which passes successfully through these trials ordained by Providence, the Almighty will in the end bestow the laurel wreath of victory.

No matter what happens, this people must and will be German.

The decisive military turning point on the Eastern Front came with the battle of Kursk, the largest tank battle in history, in the summer of 1943. Yet, the German defeat at the southern Russian city Stalingrad in the winter of 1943 was a

crucial psychological rupture, as some of the following let-
ters from German soldiers, flown out on the last plane from
the besieged city reveal. In Stalingrad, 150,000 German sol-
diers died, and the remaining 91,000 were taken prisoner by
the Soviet Army. One soldier described the dead.

You were supposed to die heroically, inspiringly, movingly, from inner conviction and for a great cause. But what is death in reality here? Here they croak, starve to death, freeze to death—it's nothing but a biological fact like eating and drinking. They drop like flies; nobody cares and nobody buries them. Without arms or legs and without eyes, with bellies torn open, they lie around everywhere.

An officer wrote to his wife about the useless and unneces-
sary suffering caused by Hitler's refusal to allow the German
troops in Stalingrad to withdraw.

I love you very much and you love me, so you will know the truth. . . . The truth is the knowledge that this is the grimmest of struggles in a hopeless situation. Misery, hunger, cold, renunciation, doubt, despair and horrible death. . . what I wrote above is no complaint or lament but a statement of objective fact.

I cannot deny my share of personal guilt in all this. . . . I am not cowardly, only sad that I cannot give greater proof of courage than to die for this useless, not to say criminal, cause.

Another soldier who had been a member of the Hitler Youth
complained to his sister that the disaster of Stalingrad had
made most of his comrades doubt Hitler's leadership.

The Führer made a firm promise to bail us out of here. . . and we believed it. . . all my life, at least eight years of it, I believed in the Führer and his word. It is terrible how they doubt here, and shameful to listen to what they say. . . because they have the facts on their side. If what we were promised is not true, then Germany will be lost, for in that case no more promises can be kept.

Slave Labor for the German War Effort

After Stalingrad, German military and civilian authorities
could no longer deny that the war on the Eastern Front was
going to last much longer than they had originally expected.

A "total war" effort would be required to beat the Russians and millions of workers would be needed to build tanks and planes. A report from a German mail censorship office in November 1942 describes how Soviet citizens were forcibly rounded up and deported to Germany as slave laborers.

Men and women, including teenagers aged 15 and above, [are being] picked up on the street, at open-air markets and village celebrations and then speeded away. The inhabitants, for that reason, are frightened, stay hidden inside, and avoid going out into public. According to the letters perused, the application of flogging as a punishment has been supplemented since about the beginning of October by the burning down of farmsteads or entire villages as a reprisal for failure to heed the orders given to the local townships for making manpower available. Implementation of this latter measure has been reported from a whole series of localities.

The racist attitudes of the German authorities and the belief that there was an endless supply of labor in the East from which to draw new recruits meant that forced laborers were treated very badly. A report filed in September 1944 by the Army Supreme Command, the leading military authority, after Hitler, described the conditions of Russian prisoner-of-war (POW) work gangs in German coal mines.

1) POWs are flogged.
2) POWs were forced to work standing in water without rubber boots.
3) POWs were lacking a second blanket, even at the end of October 1943.
4) Their quarters are frequently overcrowded, infested with vermin, and a quiet night's sleep is by no means certain.
5) POWs come with wet clothes from the pits and return to the pits with wet clothing, since there is no opportunity for drying of clothing in their quarters.
6) The examination to determine whether they are fit for work in the mines is very superficial. A civilian doctor, for example, examines up to 200 prisoners an hour as to their fitness for work.
7) Extremely high incidence of accidents. Shifts frequently go down into the shaft without a German skilled workman present among the POWs. Regulations on accident prevention are posted only in the German language.

A young man from occupied Russia works in a German war plant in 1943. By the end of the war, the Nazis had brought to Germany more than 7 million foreign laborers, most against their will. Without these men and women, Germany would have been compelled to end the war much earlier than 1945.

8) Food is available in sufficient quantity but is frequently mediocre in quality.

9) Sick persons are often not brought to the doctor promptly.

10) Sick POWs still in need of care and treatment are released and sent back into the pits prematurely.

Resistance and Invasion

In several of the countries occupied by the German Army, armed resistance to Hitler's war began to develop even before Stalingrad signaled the possibility of a German defeat. In Germany itself, the most significant resistance to Nazism during the war came not from Germans but the Russian POWs inside the Reich. But even in the heartland of Nazism some Germans began to see that continuation of Hitler's war spelled disaster. A month after the Allied invasion of Normandy on June 6, 1944, a group of high-ranking officers and other members of the German elite actually tried, but failed, to assassinate Hitler. In 1943, a group of young students in Munich, known as the White Rose resistance circle, distributed illegal pamphlets, including this appeal to the German people. The circle was a non-violent resistance group whose main aim was to convince ordinary Germans to stop supporting the Nazi regime.

A Call to All Germans!

The war is approaching its destined end...in the East the armies are constantly in retreat and invasion is imminent in the

Leading figures of the White Rose group, a student-run movement that advocated non-violent resistance to the Nazi regime. The members of this group paid with their lives after they were betrayed to the Gestapo.

When you ride ALONE you ride with Hitler!

Join a Car-Sharing Club TODAY!

An American poster appeals to civilians to economize on gasoline because it was urgently needed for the war effort. Allied victory in the Second World War depended heavily on the massive amounts of raw materials and manufactured goods supplied by the United States.

West. Mobilization in the United States has not yet reached its climax, but already it exceeds anything that the world has ever seen. It has become a mathematical certainty that Hitler is leading the German people into the abyss. Hitler cannot win the war; he can only prolong it. The guilt of Hitler and his minions has gone beyond all measure. Retribution comes closer and closer! But what are the German people doing? They will not see and will not listen. Blindly they follow their seducers into ruin. Victory at any price! is inscribed on their banner. "I will fight to the last man," says Hitler but in the meantime the war has already been lost.

Germans! Do you and your children want to suffer the same fate that befell the Jews? Do you want to be judged by the same standards as your traducers? Are we to be forever the nation which is hated and rejected by all mankind? No. Dissociate yourselves from the National Socialist gangsterism. Prove by your deeds that you think otherwise.... Make the decision before it is too late! Do not believe the National Socialist propaganda which has driven the fear of Bolshevism into your bones. Do not believe that Germany's welfare is linked to the victory of National Socialism for good or ill. A criminal regime cannot achieve a German victory. Separate yourselves in time from everything connected with National Socialism. In the aftermath a terrible but just judgment will be meted out to those who stayed in hiding, who were cowardly and hesitant.

What can we learn from the outcome of this war-this war that never was a national war?

The imperialist ideology of force, from whatever side it comes, must be shattered for all time. A one-sided Prussian militarism must never again be allowed to assume power. Only in large-scale cooperation among the nations of Europe can the ground be prepared for reconstruction.... The Germany of the future must be a federal state. At this juncture only a sound federal system can imbue a weakened Europe with a new life. The workers must be liberated from their condition of downtrodden slavery under National Socialism.... Every nation and each man have a right to the goods of the whole world!

Freedom of speech, freedom of religion, the protection of individual citizens from the arbitrary will of criminal regimes of violence—these will be the bases of the New Europe.

Support the resistance. Distribute the leaflets!

The massive Allied invasion of Normandy on June 6, 1944, put an end to Hitler's control of Western Europe. Less than a year later, on May 8, 1945, the war in Europe was over. As

early as July 15, 1944, slightly more than a month after the Allied invasion, one of Hitler's top generals, Field Marshal Erwin Rommel, wrote to Hitler that the German military position in France was desperate.

The situation on the Normandy Front is becoming more difficult every day.

As a result of the fierceness of the fighting, the extremely large amounts of materiel used by the enemy, particularly in terms of artillery and tanks, and the impact of the enemy air force which is in absolute control of the combat area, our own losses are so high that they seriously reduce the operational effectiveness of our divisions. Replacements from the homeland are few and, owing to the difficult transport situation, only reach the front after several weeks. Compared with the loss of approximately 97,000 men, including 2,160 officers and among them 28 generals and 354 commanding officers, i.e. on average 2,500-3,000 men per day, we have so far received only 6,000 men. The losses of materiel by the troops in action are also extremely high and only a small amount can be replaced, e.g. out of 225 tanks only 17.

The new divisions which have been sent are inexperienced in combat and, in view of the small amount of artillery and anti-tank weapons at their disposal, are in the long run incapable of successfully repulsing major offensives which are preceded by several hours of artillery bombardment and heavy air attacks. As has been demonstrated by the battles so far, even the bravest troops are destroyed piecemeal by the amount of materiel employed by the enemy.

The supply situation is so difficult, because of the destruction of the railway network and the vulnerability of the roads to air

Allied troops wade ashore in Normandy, France, on June 6, 1944. The invasion of northern France, combined with the advance of the Soviet army into Poland and then into Germany itself, finally destroyed the Nazi war machine.

attack up to 150 kilometres behind the front, that only the most necessary supplies can be brought up and we have to economize carefully, especially on artillery and mortar ammunition. We can no longer send significant numbers of new troops to the Normandy front. The enemy front line units, on the other hand, receive new forces and supplies of war material every day. Our Air Force has no effect on the enemy supply lines. The pressure of the enemy is becoming greater and greater.

In these circumstances, we must assume that the enemy will succeed in the foreseeable future—a fortnight to three weeks—in breaking through our own front line, above all, that held by the 7th Army, and will go forward deep into France. The consequences will be incalculable.

The Air War against Germany

During the Second World War, the British and American air forces dropped some 2.7 million tons of bombs on German territory, mainly on German cities. Between July 25 and August 3, 1943, three thousand British and American planes launched seven different attacks against just one city, the northern port city Hamburg, creating a massive firestorm. At least forty-two thousand people were killed. The police chief of Hamburg reported on these raids.

Overall, the destruction is so devastating that, in the case of many people, there is literally nothing left of them. On the basis of a layer of ashes in a large air raid shelter, doctors could only provide a rough estimate of the number of people who died there, a figure of 250-300... The horrific scenes which occurred in the area of the firestorm are indescribable. Children were torn from the hands of their parents by the tornado and whirled into the flames. People who thought they had saved themselves collapsed in a few minutes in the overwhelmingly destructive force of the heat.

A German who was a teenage boy when the 1943 Hamburg air raid took place described the injured and the dead in an oral history interview he gave in 1989.

phosphorous canisters

Incendiary devices containing a chemical element that catches fire easily

When the phosphorous canisters hit the houses, this phosphorous stuff ran down the stairs and out into the street.... The people ran out of these houses like living torches, and the flames on their bodies were put out by whoever could help them. The badly burned had to be taken away in trucks or ambulances...the drivers had to be careful that the phosphorous didn't get under their tires—the rubber burned immediately...The local hospitals, were of course, quickly filled with burn victims...Most of the people died; it was impossible for so many injured to get the proper treatment. There was no option but to bury them in mass graves.

We had to see to it that the corpses were removed as quickly as possible to prevent epidemics from spreading. The bodies were often so badly mutilated that it was impossible to identify them. Many of them had died under collapsed buildings. We dug out the ones we knew or suspected were still trapped in their cellars...Although we did all we could, many people suffocated from smoke inhalation, carbon monoxide poisoning. At one point I found a basement shelter that was full of smoke. The people sat totally still against the wall, no one made a peep. I thought my eyes were deceiving me, but they were all dead.

German women clear rubble from bombed-out buildings in Berlin. By the end of the war, American and British bombs had destroyed large areas of every major German city.

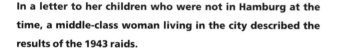

In a letter to her children who were not in Hamburg at the time, a middle-class woman living in the city described the results of the 1943 raids.

All women and children had to be evacuated from the city within six hours. There was no gas, no electricity, not a drop of water... It is hard to imagine the panic and chaos. Each one for himself, only one idea: flight....No trains could leave from Hamburg because all the stations had been gutted, and so Harburg was the nearest. There were no trams, no underground, no rail-traffic to the suburbs. Most people loaded some belongings on carts, bicycles, prams or carried things on their backs and started on foot just to get away, to escape...During the night, the suburbs of Hamm, Hammerbrock, Rothenburgsort and Barmbeck had been almost razed to the ground. People who had fled from collapsing bunkers and had got stuck in huge crowds in the streets had burning phosphorus poured over them, rushed into the next air raid shelter and were shot in order not to spread the flames.

Chapter Six

The Holocaust

When Soviet troops entered Poland and the British and Americans crossed the western German border, they encountered horrific scenes of mass death in German concentration camps. The piles of corpses that the Germans had not been able to burn made it very clear that during the war the Nazis had conducted an enormous campaign of mass murder claiming the lives of millions of Jews, Gypsies (Sinti and Roma), Poles, Russians, and other victims.

By the time Germany went to war in 1939, German Jews were already socially dead. But the Nazis did not yet dare to annihilate physically all the Jews under their control. World War II allowed the Nazis to move to the final stage of their anti-Semitic policy—physical extermination. Poland and the occupied areas of the Soviet Union now became bloody killing fields. When the German Army invaded the Soviet Union in 1941, death squads called *Einsatzgruppen* followed close behind the advancing troops, rounding up entire villages of Jews and shooting thousands of men, women, and children in cold blood. Although the *Einsatzgruppen* eventually murdered more than two million Jews, the Nazis began to search for more efficient ways of systematically implementing their plan for mass murder.

In September 1941, Zyklon B poison gas was tested on prisoners at the concentration camp Auschwitz. On December 8, 1941, the Nazis began the first mass gassings at the Chelmno extermination camp, in western Poland, where Jews were placed in mobile gas vans and driven to a burial place while carbon monoxide from the engine exhaust was fed into the sealed rear compartment. Belzec, Sobibor, Treblinka II, and Lublin-Majdanek in Poland were also developed as extermination centers. Jews were murdered by immediate gassing upon arrival or by "extermination through work." Through a combination of mass

Two starved inmates in the Nordhausen concentration camp liberated by American troops. When advancing American soldiers overran German concentration camps in the spring of 1945, they were shocked by the piles of bodies they found and by the deplorable physical conditions of the inmates who were still alive. American newspapers quickly published pictures such as this one, exposing millions of American civilians to horrific images of the Holocaust.

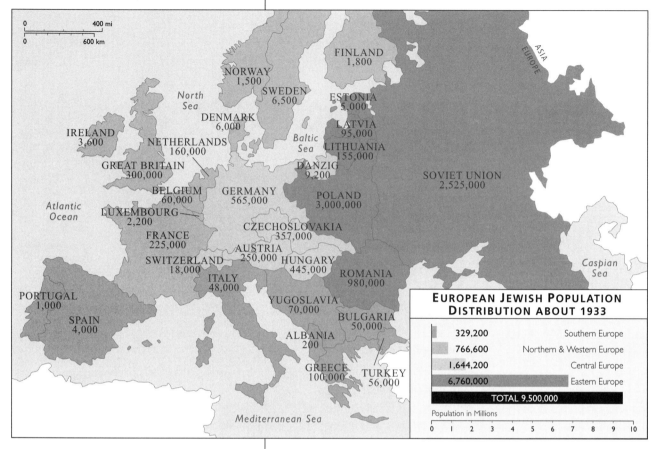

EUROPEAN JEWISH POPULATION DISTRIBUTION ABOUT 1933	
329,200	Southern Europe
766,600	Northern & Western Europe
1,644,200	Central Europe
6,760,000	Eastern Europe
TOTAL 9,500,000	

Population in Millions
0 1 2 3 4 5 6 7 8 9 10

In 1933 most of Europe's Jewish population lived in Eastern Europe, and Poland had the largest number of Jewish citizens. The entire Jewish population of Europe was about 9.5 million, more than 60 percent of the world's Jewish population at the time. It has been estimated that by the time the war ended in May 1945, the Nazis had murdered as many as 68 percent of all the Jews in Western and Eastern Europe, including the Soviet Union.

shootings, gassings, and working Jews to death, the Nazis murdered between 4,194,200 and 5,721,00 Jewish citizens of some nineteen different European nations before they were stopped by defeat in the spring of 1945.

The Nazis also deported Sinti and Roma families to camps in the East. Of the twenty-three thousand Roma sent to Auschwitz, at least nineteen thousand died as a result of disease, starvation, or execution. Before the war approximately one million Roma lived in Europe. The Nazis killed at least 220,000 of them. Thousands of homosexual men convicted under Paragraph 175 of the Nazi criminal code were imprisoned in concentration camps. Overwork, starvation, physical brutality, and murder ensured high death rates for gays in the camps.

The First Steps toward Mass Murder

As the German Army conquered large areas of Western and Eastern Europe, millions of European Jews came under German control. In Hitler's perverted view of the world, these

Jews were a deadly threat and had to be eliminated. In a speech to the German Reichstag in January 1939, Hitler foreshadowed the coming genocide, the deliberate murder of an entire race of people or nation.

In the course of my life I have very often been a prophet, and have usually been ridiculed for it. During the time of my struggle for power it was in the first instance only the Jewish race that received my prophecies with laughter when I said that I would one day take over the leadership of the State, and with it that of the whole nation, and that I would then among other things settle the Jewish problem. Their laughter was uproarious, but I think that for some time now they have been laughing on the other side of their face.

Today I will once more be a prophet: if the international Jewish financiers in and outside Europe should succeed in plunging the nations once more into a world war, then the result will not be the Bolshevizing of the earth, and thus the victory of Jewry, but the annihilation of the Jewish race in Europe!

"Aryan Germans," not Jews, were the first victims of the Nazis' wartime campaign to murder innocent civilians. Hitler ordered the killing of large numbers of "biologically unworthy" Aryan Germans, starting with infants then moving on to adults. The Nazis called these murders euthanasia, which means mercy killing, suggesting that they were putting the mentally or physically disabled out of their misery. In reality, this was the cruel and cynical murder of people whom the Nazis considered a burden to the war effort. In testimony given after the war, a man who worked at the Hartheim killing center in Austria described how the patients were gassed.

I began work at Hartheim on 2 April 1940...

About six weeks after the 2 April 1940, the preparations and the buildings were ready and the plant began to operate. The mentally ill were, as far as I know, brought from the various asylums by train and bus to Hartheim at very different times of the day... The numbers arriving varied between 40 and 150. First, they were taken to the undressing room. There

A letter signed by Hitler in September 1939 authorizes the T4 program to murder Germans suffering from incurable physical and mental diseases or other conditions the Nazis considered to be hereditary. The Nazis hid their intentions behind the innocent-sounding label T4, the initials of the building in Berlin (Tiergartenstrasse 4) where Nazi officials administered the euthanasia program.

they—men and women in different sections—had to undress or were undressed. Their clothes and luggage were put in a pile, labelled, registered and numbered. The people who had undressed then went along a passage into the so-called reception room. In this room there was a large table. A doctor was there together with a staff of 3–4 assistants.... As far as I can judge as a layman, the doctors did not examine these people but only checked their files. Someone then stamped them. An orderly had to stamp them individually on the shoulder or the chest with a consecutive number. The number was approximately 3–4 cm in size. Those people who had gold teeth or a gold bridge were marked with a cross on their backs. After this procedure, the people were led into a nearby room and photographed. Then the people were led out of the photography room through a second exit back into the reception room and from there through a steel door into the gas chamber.

The gas chamber had a very bare interior. It had a wooden floor and there were wooden benches in the chamber. Later, the floor was concreted and finally it and the walls were tiled. The ceiling and the other parts of the walls were painted with oil. The whole room was designed to give the impression that it was a bathroom. Three showers were fixed in the ceiling. The room was aired by ventilators. A window in the gas chamber was covered with a grill. A second steel door led into the room where the gassing apparatus was installed.

When the whole transport had been dealt with, i.e. when the registration had been carried out, the photographs taken, people's numbers stamped on them, and those with gold teeth marked, they all went into the bath-gas room. The steel doors were shut and the doctor on duty fed gas into the gas chamber. After a short time the people in the gas chamber were dead. After around an hour and a half, the gas chamber was ventilated. At this point, we burners had to start work.

To complete the process of separating Jews from non-Jews and to make it easier for the authorities to deport Jews to the extermination camps in the East, the Nazis made all Jews wear the so-called Jewish star. In his secret diary, Victor Klemperer described the humiliating experience of wearing the star. He does not go out during the day because he is worried about how he will be treated now that he is forced to wear the star. His wife, Eva, does not have to wear the star because she is an Aryan German.

In Germany, the requirement that Jews wear the yellow Jewish star labeled with the German word for Jew marked the final phase of their isolation from the rest of the society. The next step was deportation and annihilation.

September 18, Thursday evening
The "Jewish star," black on yellow cloth, at the center in Hebrew-like lettering "Jew," to be worn on the left breast, large as the palm of a hand, issued to us yesterday for 10 pfennigs [pennies], to be worn from tomorrow. The omnibus [a vehicle for transporting large numbers of people] may *no* longer be used, *only* the front platform of the tram.— For the time being at least Eva will take over all the shopping, I shall breathe in a little fresh air only under shelter of darkness…

September 20, Saturday
Yesterday, as Eva was sewing on the Jew's star, I had a raving fit of despair. Eva's nerves [are] finished too. She is pale, her cheeks are hollow. (The day before yesterday, for the first time in years, we had ourselves weighed. Eva was 123 pounds, six and a half pounds lighter than in the turnip winter of 1917—her normal weight was 154 pounds. I am still 148 pounds—it was 165 pounds before.)…Yesterday after the evening meal a few steps outside with Eva only when it was completely dark. Today at midday I really did go to Olsner's grocery shop…and fetched soda water. It cost me a great effort to do so. Meanwhile Eva is constantly going on errands and cooking. Our whole life has been turned upside down, and everything weighs on Eva. How long will her feet hold out?—She visited Frau Kronheim. The latter took the tram yesterday—front platform. The driver: Why was she not sitting in the car? Frau Kronheim is small, slight, stooped, her hair completely white. As a Jewess she was forbidden to do so. The driver struck the panel with his fist: "What a mean thing!" Poor comfort.

Two Belgian Jewish children pose for a photograph in 1942. At six years old, the girl was either too young to be required to wear the Jewish star that is sewn onto her brother's sweater or it is hidden under her apron.

The War against Eastern Jews

By the time the decree requiring German Jews to wear the star went into effect, mobile killing squads (*Einsatzgruppen*) were already beginning to murder Jews in eastern Poland

and the parts of the Soviet Union conquered by the German Army. Between September 29 and 30, 1941, SS *Einsatzgruppen* murdered 33,771 Jews at Babi Yar ravine, near Kiev (captial of the Soviet Ukraine). Dina Pronicheva, a Jewish resident of the area, described how she managed to survive the Babi Yar mass executions.

It was dark already... They lined us up on a ledge which was so small that we couldn't get much of a footing on it.

They began shooting us. I shut my eyes, clenched my fists, tensed all my muscles and took a plunge down before the bullets hit me. It seemed I was flying forever. But I landed safely on the bodies. After a while, when the shooting stopped, I heard the

A member of a Nazi killing squad stands ready to shoot a Ukranian Jew who has been forced to kneel at the edge of a mass grave. The German who took this picture probably believed that his camera was recording not a horrific crime but a great event.

Germans climbing into the ravine. They started finishing off all those who were not dead yet, those who were moaning, hiccuping, tossing, writhing in agony. They ran their flashlights over the bodies and finished off all who moved. I was lying so still without stirring, terrified of giving myself away. I felt I was done for. I decided to keep quiet. They started covering the corpses over with earth. They must have put quite a lot over me because I felt I was beginning to suffocate. But I was afraid to move. I was gasping for breath. I knew I would suffocate. Then I decided it was better to be shot than buried alive. I stirred but I didn't know that it was quite dark already. Using my left arm I managed to move a little way up. Then I took a deep breath, summoned up my waning strength and crawled out from under the cover of earth. It was dark. But all the same it was dangerous to crawl because of the searching beams of flashlight and they continued shooting at those who moaned. They might hit me. So I had to be careful. I was lucky enough to crawl up one of the high walls of the ravine, and straining every nerve and muscle, got out of it.

Those Jews not immediately murdered by the *Einsatzgruppen* were forced into ghettos until the Nazis decided that they no longer needed any of them to perform forced labor for the Nazi war effort. The Nazis established the biggest ghetto in occupied Europe in Warsaw, the capital of Poland. More than 350,000 Jews lived in Warsaw—30 percent of the city's entire population—making this the largest single Jewish community in Europe. On October 12, 1940, the Germans announced that all Jews in Warsaw would have to move into an area of the capital surrounded by a closely guarded wall more than ten-feet high, topped with barbed wire. Crammed into massively overcrowded, unhygienic dwellings and officially allowed far less than starvation rations, Jews died in large numbers from malnutrition and disease. The diary of a visitor, Stanislav Rozycki, describes the conditions in the ghetto.

The majority are nightmare figures, ghosts of former human beings, miserable destitutes, pathetic remnants of former humanity. One is most affected by the characteristic change which one sees in their faces: as a result of misery, poor nourishment, the lack of vitamins, fresh air and exercise, the numerous cares, worries, anticipated misfortunes, suffering and sickness, their faces have taken on a skeletal appearance. The prominent bones around their

In the Jewish residential district there are around 27,000 apartments with an average of 2 1/2 rooms each. This produces an occupation density of 15.1 persons per apartment and 6–7 persons per room.

—Waldemar Schön, director of the Resettlement Department attached to the Nazi governor of the Warsaw district, reporting in January 1941, about the creation of the Warsaw ghetto.

eye sockets, the yellow facial colour, the slack pendulous skin, the alarming emaciation and sickliness. And, in addition, this miserable, frightened, restless, apathetic and resigned expression like that of a hunted animal. I pass my closest friends without recognising them and guessing their fate...

On the streets children are crying in vain, children who are dying of hunger. They howl, beg, sing, moan, shiver with cold, without underwear, without clothing, without shoes, in rags, sacks, flannel which are bound in strips round the emaciated skeletons, children swollen with hunger, disfigured, half conscious, already completely grown-up at the age of five, gloomy and weary of life. They are like old people and are only conscious of one thing: "I'm cold," "I'm hungry"... Ten per cent of the new generation have already perished: every day and every night hundreds of these children die and there is no hope that anybody will put a stop to it...

For various reasons standards of hygiene are terribly poor. Above all, the fearful population density in the streets with which nowhere in Europe can be remotely compared. The fatal over-pop-

In Poland's Warsaw ghetto, people walk past the bodies of those who have died from starvation or disease. The residents of the Warsaw ghetto had to survive on an official food allocation of 300 calories per day.

ulation is particularly apparent in the streets: people literally rub against each other, it is impossible to pass unhindered through the streets. And then the lack of light, gas, and heating materials. Water consumption is also much reduced; people wash themselves much less and do not have baths or hot water. There are no green spaces, gardens, parks: no clumps of trees and no lawns to be seen. For a year no one has seen a village, a wood, a field, a river or a mountain: no one has breathed slightly better air for even a few days this year. Bedding and clothing are changed very rarely because of the lack of soap. To speak of food hygiene would be a provocation and would be regarded as mockery. People eat what is available, however much is available and when it is available. Other principles of nutrition are unknown here. Having said all this, one can easily draw one's own conclusions as to the consequences: stomach typhus and typhus, dysentery, tuberculosis, pneumonia, influenza, metabolic disturbances, the most common digestive illnesses, lack of vitamins and all other illnesses associated with the lack of bread, fresh air, clothing, and heating materials. Typhus is systematically and continually destroying the population. There are victims in every family. On average up to a thousand people are dying each month. In the early morning the corpses of beggars, children, old people, young people and women are lying in every street—the victims of the hunger and the cold.

Killing Centers

Even if Jews managed to survive the horrific conditions of the ghettos, they were unlikely to escape the periodic mass deportations from the ghettos to extermination centers such as Auschwitz. In the fall of 1942, for example, the Nazis deported about 300,000 Jews from the Warsaw ghetto to the Treblinka II death camp. And as the Nazi grip tightened over all of occupied Europe, Jews were also deported from every corner of the continent directly to the death camps in Poland. These deportations to the East were themselves instruments of murder. Bart Stern was born in Hungary in 1926. In 1944, he was deported to Auschwitz. In a 1992 interview, Stern described the conditions he had to endure during this three-day trip.

We were pushed up on railroad cars, actually cattle cars. But the amazing thing, what I still remember is, that on the way, being driven, or herded, by the Hungarian gendarmes, we were singing

Hungarian Jews arrive in Auschwitz-Birkenau concentration camp in Poland the spring of 1944. Nearly 440,000 Jews were deported from Hungary to Auschwitz in the spring and summer of that year. Most of them were murdered in the gas chambers immediately after their arrival.

so . . . songs of hope. I do not remember exactly how to translate the song but I know where, which part of the Psalms it is in. And we thought that we are already enough in it [the cattle car]. We were about 50 people or 60. Twenty more, 30 more, so we must have been in that little cattle car, which is about a third of the size of an American railroad car, about 120, 140. And before we knew, whoever didn't make it of the family in the same car was cut off and they, they just slammed the doors, and those who were outside, they still had to put barbed wire on the little bit of opening which was on the outside on the top of the railroad car.

These car[s] were usually used for cattle transports or for grain. In the car the situation got by the minute worse and worse. People were looking to find a spot for the older . . . elder people to sit down. There was no space to sit down, because if you sat down you couldn't get up, because we were herded in, squeezed like in a sardine box. The journey actually lasted—Tuesday, Wednesday, Thursday—three nights and about three days. If anybody had something to eat—because in the ghettos we already used up most of the stuff what we have been successful taking out of our homes when we were taken out into the ghetto—had to share it with others. But we realized that it is not a simple journey of just a few hours. People were holding back, or they couldn't as generously pass it out to others. Then suddenly we start seeing that people are taking care of their needs in the cars, and the stench got worse every minute.

The SS normally gassed women with young children, old people, and people with physical infirmities upon arrival at Auschwitz. Only healthy boys, relatively young men and some women judged capable of work were spared, though temporarily. The Nazis intended to kill these Jews by giving them too little food and making them perform hard physical labor that would wear them out within a few months. Periodic selections also condemned to death those inmates judged no longer fit to work. In a 1990 interview, Fritzie Weiss Fritzshall, a Jewish woman born in 1929 in Klucarky, Czechoslovakia, described the selection process in Auschwitz.

We needed to show that we still had strength left, to, whether it was to work or to live another day. I recall some women, um, were beginning as their hair grows back, they were beginning to get gray hair, and they would go and take a little piece of coal from one of the pot-bellied stoves that was in a barrack. And they would use this coal to color their hair with so that they would look a, a little younger. I mean one grayed at the age of maybe eighteen or nineteen under those conditions. And they would run... we would run in front of whoever it was that was doing the selections to show that we could survive one other day. If one had a scar, a pimple, if one didn't run fast enough, if one didn't look right for whatever reason to the particular person that was doing the selection—they would stand there with a stick, to the right or to the left, as you ran by them. One never knew if they were in the good line or the bad

A prisoner's jacket worn by Abraham Lewent, who was deported from the Warsaw ghetto to the Majdanek camp near Lublin, Poland. Lewent was later sent to several other concentration camps in Germany and was issued this jacket when he arrived in Buchenwald concentration camp in 1944.

An invoice for Zyklon B, the pesticide used in some concentration camp gas chambers, submitted to Kurt Gerstein. Gerstein was an SS officer who secretly collected evidence of the Nazi extermination of the Jews in the Auschwitz and Belzec concentration camps. Although he wanted to act as a witness against Nazi war criminals, Gerstein himself came under suspicion after the end of World War II and committed suicide in July 1945.

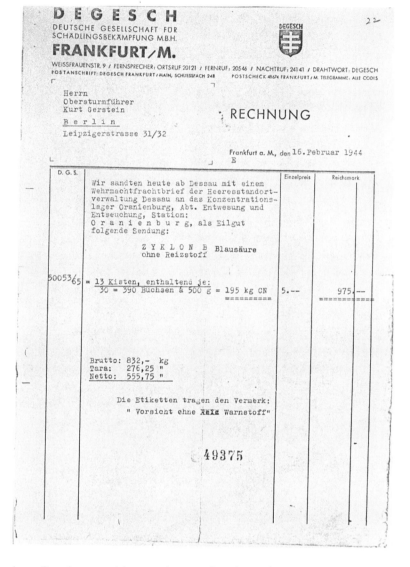

line. One line would go to the gas chambers, the other line would go back to the camp and to the barracks to live another day.

Kurt Gerstein claimed to have joined the SS to gather evidence on the mass murders in the extermination centers. As a trained engineer, he was responsible for distributing and supervising the use of chemicals in the camps. In 1942, he was sent to deliver prussic acid (one of the poisons used in the gas chambers) to the commandants of Belzec, Treblinka, and Sobibor. At the end of the war, he was captured by the Allies. In a deposition to Allied military officers in May 1945, Gerstein described a gassing he had observed in Belzec. He committed suicide shortly afterward.

We left for Belzec two days later. . . .

Next morning, a few minutes before seven, I was told: "In ten minutes the first train will arrive!" Indeed, a few minutes later a train arrived from Lemberg [a city in western Ukraine], with 45 cars holding 6,700 people, of whom 1,450 were already dead on arrival. Behind the small barbed-wired window, children, young ones, frightened to death, women, men. The train pulled in: 200 Ukrainians detailed for the task wrenched open the doors and with their leather whips drove the Jews out of the cars. A loudspeaker issued instructions: to remove all clothing, even artificial limbs and eyeglasses; to tie their shoes together with small pieces of string handed out by a little Jewish boy; to turn in all valuables, all money at the ticket window "Valuables," without voucher, without receipt. Women and girls were to have their hair cut off in the "Barber's" barrack. (An SS sergeant on duty told me: "That's to make something special for submarine crews, for packaging or something like that.")

Then the march began. To the left and right, barbed wire; behind, two dozen Ukrainians, guns in hand. They approached. [Captain] Wirth and I, we were standing on the ramp in front of the death chambers. Completely nude, men, women, young girls, children, babies, cripples, filed by. At the corner stood a heavy SS man, who told the poor people, in a pastoral voice: "No harm will come to you! You just have to breathe very deeply, that strengthens the lungs, inhaling is a means of preventing contagious diseases. It's a good disinfection!" They asked what was going to happen to them. He told them: "The men will have to work, building roads and houses. But the women won't be obliged to do so; they'll do housework, cooking." For some of these poor creatures, this was a last small hope, enough to carry them, unresisting, as far as the death chambers. Most of them knew all, the odor confirmed it! They walked up the small wooden flight of stairs and entered the death chambers, most without a word, pushed forward by those behind them. One Jewish woman of about forty, her eyes flaming torches, cursed the murderers; after several whiplashes by Captain Wirth in person, she disappeared into the gas chamber.

Pollo R., a young Roma boy deported to Auschwitz, described his feelings upon arriving at the death camp.

Longingly I looked at the gate which barred my way out of the compound filled with screaming humanity. Near me on several trucks were hundreds of nude men, women, and children.

In less than ten minutes all the fit men had been collected together in a group. What happened to the others, to the women, to the children, to the old men, we could establish neither then nor later: the night swallowed them up, purely and simply.

—Author Primo Levi describing his arrival at an extermination camp in his 1958 book, *Survival in Auschwitz*

Although they had not been on my transport, like me they were Gypsies, only they were from Silesia. I could hear and understand their prayers in Romany. They implored God (but in vain) to spare at least their children's lives. I was only fourteen at the time, and now realize that I had no real understanding of the situation I was witnessing. But instinctively I knew that something unimaginable was going to happen.

We were told to line up quickly. Those that lagged a bit were hit with batons. One SS guard barked at us as he pointed toward the chimney stacks which seemed to reach for the sky like long threatening fingers, "This will be *your* way out of Auschwitz!"

Born in the north German city of Lübeck, Friedrich-Paul von Groszheim had trained to be a merchant. He describes the Nazis persecution of him as a gay man.

In January 1937 the SS arrested 230 men in Luebeck [a city in northern Germany] under the Nazi-revised criminal code's paragraph 175, which outlawed homosexuality, and I was imprisoned for 10 months. The Nazis had been using paragraph 175 as

Silesia

A central European region, most of which is now within the borders of Poland

Roma, or Gypsy, prisoners sit outdoors awaiting instructions in Belzec, a Polish concentration camp, in 1940. The Germans and their allies killed between 25 and 50 percent of the approximately one million Roma living in Europe before the war.

grounds for making mass arrests of homosexuals. In 1938 I was re-arrested, humiliated, and tortured. The Nazis finally released me, but only on the condition that I agree to be castrated. I submitted to the operation... Because of the nature of my operation, I was rejected as "physically unfit" when I came up for military service in 1940. In 1943 I was arrested again, this time for being a monar-chist, a supporter of the former Kaiser Wilhelm II. The Nazis imprisoned me as a political prisoner in an annex of the Neuengamme concentration camp at Luebeck.

Rescue, Escape, and Resistance

After the Nazis had occupied most of continental Western Europe, it was still possible for Jews to escape Hitler's grasp if they could get help from a rescue committee or from a representative of a foreign government who was willing to issue them an entry visa. Varian Fry, an American who went to France in 1940 as a representative of a private agency, the Emergency Rescue Committee, was one of the people who worked to rescue European Jews. Fry managed to save or help thousands of refugees who were being hunted by the Gestapo, including many prominent Jewish intellectuals and artists, including the Russian painter Marc Chagall and the German political scientist Hannah Arendt. In his memoir, Fry describes some of the work he did in the thirteen months before he was deported by the Vichy French authorities.

At the end of January [1941] many of the refugees discovered they could get exit visas... the immediate result for us was that from having been ostensibly a modest relief organization, paying small weekly allowances to keep men, women and children from starving to death, ours now quickly became a kind of travel bureau... For we could now openly engage in what had all along been our rai-son d'etre—emigration.

It took us a little while to get used to the change, but by the end of the first week we had already adjusted to it, and for the first time since we began work, more than five months before, we were soon sending refugees down to the Spanish frontier to leave France legally...

It was the ships to Martinique which really kept us busy. We couldn't have thought up anything better if we had had the power to arrange the route ourselves. They not only eliminated the trou-ble with the transit visas—they also removed the danger of the

Walter Meyerhof   December 17, 1940

Mr. H. Freeman Matthews,
American Embassy,
Vichy, Allier.

Dear Mr. Matthews,

        I wonder if you will be good enough to
lend your special support to Mr. Walter Meyerhof's demand
for a "sortie" visa.

        Walter is the son of Professor
Otto Meyerhof, biologist, who is now on the Faculty of
the University of Pennsylvania. Professor and Mrs. Meyerhof
left France some months ago, but Walter was not able to
accompany them as at the time he did not have his American
visa. He made his demand for a "sortie" visa and "titre
de voyage" at the Préfecture of Perpignan on December 5th. At
the Préfecture they told him that his demand had been
accepted with an "avis favorable" and that his dossier
would be at Vichy by December 10th.

        Walter passed the Kundt commission at
Le Cheylard and he is eager to leave France as soon as
possible to join his parents.

        I should be very grateful indeed to do
whatever you can to help him obtain his "sortie" visa
without a long delay.

        Yours very truly,

        Varian M. Fry
        Director.

VMF/ag.

In a 1940 letter to the American consul in Vichy France, American journalist Varian Fry asks for help in obtaining an exit visa for Walter Meyerhof, the son of a Jewish Nobel Prize winner. Fry's efforts helped hundreds of Jewish artists, scientists, and intellectuals escape Europe and almost certain death in a Nazi extermination camp.

trip through Spain. For they went directly from Marseille to Martinique, and from there it was possible to go straight to New York. They were almost as good as the much-advertised but never-realized "rescue ship," which was to have come to Marseille to take refugees to New York, but wouldn't have been able to take a single refugee on board at the time it was proposed, for at that time literally no one was able to get an exit visa...

At the end of May, when we came to tally our work, we found that in less than eight months over 15,000 people had come to us or written to us. We had had to consider every one of their cases and take a decision on it. We had decided that 1,800 of the cases fell within the scope of our activities. In other words, that they were genuine cases of intellectual or political refugees with a good chance of emigrating soon. Of these 1,800 cases, representing, in all, some 4,000 human beings, we had paid weekly living allowances to 560 and had sent more than 1,000 out of France. For the rest we had made every kind of effort, from getting them liberated from concentration camps to finding them a dentist...

But it was not everyone who could get an exit visa and leave France legally, even then. As usual, the regulations were shrouded in mystery, but we were told that every prefecture in the unoccupied zone had been provided with lists of persons to whom the visas were to be refused.

Elisabeth Freund came from an educated German Jewish family. Her uncle was a Nobel Prize winner. She studied economics in Breslau, a city which at that time was in eastern Germany, and Berlin. Like other Jews in Berlin she was forced by the Nazis to work in an armaments factory. In her 1941 memoir, she describes how she narrowly missed being

deported to a death camp by being allowed to leave for Cuba with her husband just before Himmler suspended all emigration from Germany in October 1941.

The Gestapo has permitted me to leave Germany, in spite of the prohibition. We do not even dare to believe it yet. It came about like this: My husband met an old acquaintance quite by chance on the street, an executive in one of the major banks of Berlin, with whom he had worked together a great deal, especially at the time of the uprisings in Upper Silesia after the First World War... This gentleman, then, asked quite innocently, in a friendly manner, how we were doing, and was absolutely flabbergasted when he heard what difficulties we were having. "But really, that just can't be! These measures are not meant for someone like you!" How often have we and a thousand other Jews heard these words already...

Well, at any rate, this gentleman was very sympathetic. He asked for exact details and was going to discuss the matter with the management of his company. There they had the necessary connections to the Gestapo and would somehow fix things up for us. When my husband told me about this meeting I was so pessimistic and so tired from work that I scarcely listened. After all, we had experienced so many disappointments already; why should it turn out otherwise this time? We were also very afraid and not at all so pleased by the well-meaning offer, for after all, one does not know what could happen if something like that were passed on to the wrong place.

But the miracle happened. Things turned out well... The Gestapo man who negotiated the matter, to be sure, would like to have a bed from us when we leave—that's all. And we will leave

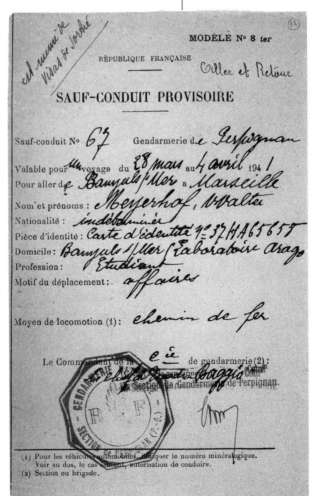

Local police in Perpignan, France, issued this safe conduct pass to Walter Meyerhof, allowing him to travel by train to Marseilles in 1941. Meyerhof was able to escape to Lisbon and from there to the United States in April 1941.

My uncle got this passeur [a guide who helped Jews escape occupied Europe] for us, and... he was going to take us to Nice, in the southern part of France. My mother paid him... the equivalent of sixty thousand dollars... but when we... left with the passeur to go back to go to the southern part of France, we went through Brussels. In the middle of the street, he left us. He had received his money and he left us. And we knew nobody in Brussels.

—Liny Pajgin Yollick describes fleeing to France from Antwerp in 1942 in a 1990 interview

him this bed with the greatest pleasure. All these things are so scarce and cannot be bought in the normal way.

But we have nothing in writing on this decision. In principle, the Gestapo does not provide anything written in such cases. My husband immediately went to the emigration office of the Jewish Aid Society. He was congratulated there, but no one wants to take the responsibility for placing our names on a departure list. One cannot blame them for that; after all, everything is punishable by immediate deportation to a concentration camp.

The best thing is to let the business of emigration simply happen, as if it did not concern us at all, as if we were acting in a film. Otherwise the tension is too difficult to bear...

For the last time we are sitting at our own table for a meal. Then we put on our coats, each one of us takes a knapsack and a small handbag, and we leave the house without looking back.

By city train we go to the Potsdam station. There, in the cellar of the station, the Jewish groups are assembled. After the examination of our papers we are let into the cellar. The door closes behind us. Thank God! The group is leaving today after all. Until the last moment we had been afraid that the journey would not be allowed. There are still many formalities with luggage and passports. We find out that last night the first groups also left Frankfurt am Main. Three hours pass until we are finally led in complete darkness through the unlit station to the train to Paris. A sealed car is designated for our group. We get in, the doors are closed, the train begins to move. We are riding to freedom.

Four days later the German government forbids departure for all Jews, and the army command discontinues the release of freight cars for the journey through France.

But the deportation of Jews to Poland goes on.

By September 1942 it was clear that the Germans intended to liquidate the Warsaw ghetto. More than 300,000 Jews had been deported to the death camps since July of that year. When the Germans tried to finish the removal of the remaining sixty thousand ghetto residents to the death camps on April 19, 1943, the eve of Passover, Jewish underground groups started an armed uprising. The fighting continued until May 16, 1943. The Germans completely destroyed the ghetto and killed or deported to the camps most of the remaining inhabitants. Despite its ultimate failure, the Warsaw uprising sent a signal to the world that some Jews in occupied Europe were not prepared to go to their

deaths without fighting back. On April 23, 1943, Mordecai Anielewicz, one of the leaders of the uprising, wrote a last letter from the ghetto to one of his friends.

It is impossible to put into words what we have been through. One thing is clear, what happened exceeded our boldest dreams. The Germans ran twice from the ghetto. One of our companies held out for 40 minutes and another—for more than 6 hours. The mine set in the "brushmakers" [a district inside the Warsaw ghetto] area exploded. Several of our companies attacked the dispersing Germans. Our losses in manpower are minimal. That is also an achievement. Y [Yechiel] fell. He fell a hero, at the machine-gun. *I feel that great things are happening and what we dared do is of great, enormous importance. . . .*

Beginning from today we shall shift over to the partisan tactic. Three battle companies will move out tonight, with two tasks: reconnaissance and obtaining arms. Do you remember, short-range weapons are of no use to us. We use such weapons only rarely. What we need urgently: grenades, rifles, machine-guns and explosives.

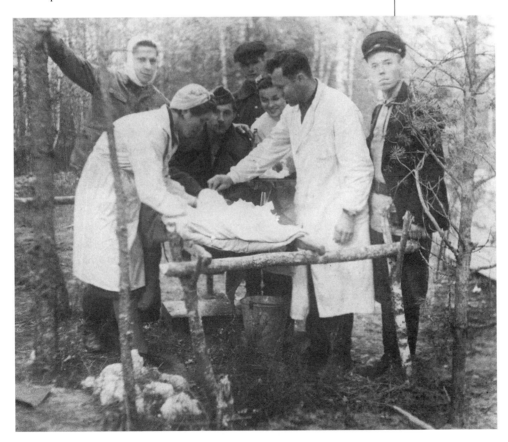

A field hospital belonging to a partisan unit in Belarus treats a wounded fighter in a forest. The woman on the left, bending over the patient, is a Jewish photographer and field nurse who escaped the Nazis to join this unit.

It is impossible to describe the conditions under which the Jews of the ghetto are now living. Only a few will be able to hold out. The remainder will die sooner or later. Their fate is decided. In almost all the hiding places in which thousands are concealing themselves it is not possible to light a candle for lack of air.

With the aid of our transmitter we heard a marvelous report on our fighting by the "Shavit" radio station. The fact that we are remembered beyond the ghetto walls encourages us in our struggle. Peace go with you, my friend! Perhaps we may still meet again! *The dream of my life has risen to become fact. Self-defense in the ghetto will have been a reality. Jewish armed resistance and revenge are facts. I have been a witness to the magnificent, heroic fighting of Jewish men of battle.*

Shavit

Hebrew word for comet. Presumably an illegal Jewish radio broadcast

Money issued by the Jewish Council of Elders in the Theresienstadt ghetto in western Czechoslovakia bears an image of Moses and the Ten Commandments.

The Nazis murdered between 4,194,200 and 5,721,00 European Jews and destroyed Jewish ways of life with centuries-old traditions. In central and eastern Europe, the cultural, religious, and ethnic terrain had been changed forever. For those who survived, the trauma of the Holocaust could never be forgotten. And the effects of the wound might even be transmitted to the next generation. In her novel *Fugitive Pieces,* Canadian author Anne Michaels describes an exchange between a Holocaust survivor who had faced starvation in one of the death camps and his son.

The memories we elude catch up to us, overtake us like a shadow...

My father found the apple in the garbage. It was rotten and I'd thrown it out—I was eight or nine. He fished it from the bin, sought me in my room, grabbed me tight by the shoulder, and pushed the apple to my face.

"What is this? What is it?" "An apple—"

My mother kept food in her purse. My father ate frequently to avoid the first twists of hunger because, once they gripped him, he'd eat until he was sick. Then he ate dutifully, methodically, tears streaming down his face, animal and spirit in such raw evidence, knowing he was degrading both. If one needs proof of the soul, it's easily found. The spirit is most evident at the point of extreme bodily humiliation. There was no pleasure, for my father, associated with food. It was years before I realized this wasn't merely a psychological difficulty, but also a moral one, for who could answer my father's question: Knowing what he knew, should he stuff himself, or starve?

"An apple! Well, my smart son, is an apple food?"

SS troops round up participants in the Warsaw Ghetto uprising in 1943. Rather than allow themselves to be shipped off to the death camps without a fight, these Jewish men and women resisted the SS troops with guns and other weapons smuggled into the ghetto.

HITLER DEAD

The German radio announced last night that Adolf Hitler had died yesterday afternoon, and that Adm. Doenitz, former commander-in-chief of the German Navy, had succeeded him as ruler of the Reich.

Doenitz, speaking later over the German radio, Reuter said, declared that "Hitler has fallen at his command post."

"My first task," Doenitz said, "is to save the German people from destruction by Bolshevism. If only for this task, the struggle will continue."

Churchill Hints Peace Is at Hand

Winston Churchill indicated in a brief address to Commons yesterday that peace in Europe might come before Saturday.

Although he declined to give any statement on the reported surrender negotiations, the Prime Minister acknowledged that an important announcement was possible before the House adjourned Friday night. The discussion was regarded as confirmation that the negotiations are well under way.

In Stockholm, meanwhile, Count Folke Bernadotte, head of the Swedish Red Cross, gave virtual denial of a press conference that he was acting as go-between in peace negotiations between the Allies and the German government.

Count Denies Visit

"I have not seen Himmler during my last visit to Germany and Denmark, and I have not forwarded any message from Himmler or any authoritative German to the ..., said the Swedish nobleman shortly after his return by plane from Copenhagen.

The count, previously had been regarded as the intermediary through

(Continued on Page 8)

Truman Names New Aide

WASHINGTON, May 1 (AP).— President Truman today appointed Edward Daniel McKim, an Omaha, Neb., insurance executive, to be his chief administrative assistant.

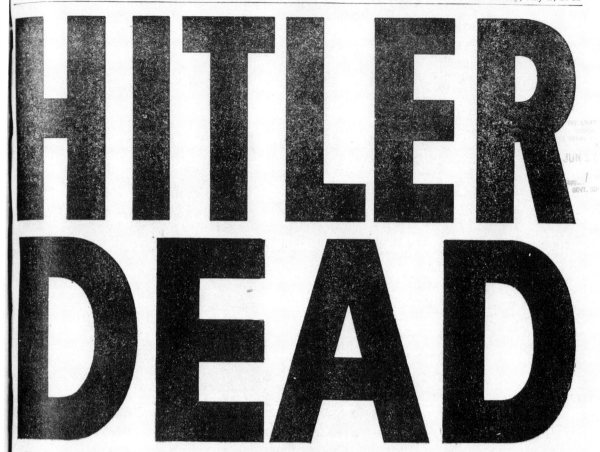

Adolf Hitler at his height

Story of Hitler's Life on Page .

The announcement preceding the proclamation by Doenitz said: "It is reported from the Fuehrer's headquarters that our Fuehrer, Adolf Hitler, has fallen this afternoon at his command post in the Reich Chancellery, fighting to the last breath against Bolshevism and for his country. On April 30, the Fuehrer appointed Grand Adm. Doenitz as his successor. The new Fuehrer will speak to the German people."

The talk by Doenitz then followed, Reuter said. Doenitz said: "German men and women, soldiers of the German Wehrmacht, our Fuehrer, Adolf Hitler, has fallen. German people are in deepest mourning and veneration."

"Adolf Hitler recognized beforehand the terrible danger of Bolshevism," Doenitz said, "and devoted his life to fighting it. At the end of this, his battle, and of his unswerving straight path of life, stands his death as a hero in the capital of the Reich.

"All his life meant service to the German people. His battle against the Bolshevik flood benefited not only Europe but the whole world. The Fuehrer has appointed me as his successor. Fully conscious of the responsibility, I take over the leadership of the Ger-

(Continued on Page 8)

Chapter Seven

Germany after the Holocaust

The war ended for Germany in complete defeat. The Allies insisted that the Germans sign an unconditional surrender, which they did in two separate ceremonies in May 1945, one in Reims, France, and the second in Berlin. In a series of wartime agreements, the Allies declared that they would occupy Germany for an unspecified period of time. Germany was divided into four zones of occupation, Soviet, American, British, and French. The Allies intended to destroy all remnants of Nazism in the country and make sure that Germany would never again start another war. In November 1945, the Allies began the Nuremberg trials, an international tribunal held in the city where the Nazis had staged their party rallies. Twenty-one defendants were indicted for conspiring to wage aggressive war and for war crimes. Ten received the death penalty, three were acquitted, and the rest got prison sentences. With the exception of Hermann Goering, none of the topmost Nazi leaders could be put on trial because they had all committed suicide—Hitler and Goebbels in a bunker in Berlin as the Russians advanced into the city, Himmler just after he was captured by the British.

By the late 1940s, the division of Germany into four separate zones of Allied occupation (Russian in the East, American, British and French in the West) had hardened into a permanent split between two new German states—West and East Germany, both founded in 1949. (Germany would remain divided until the fall of the Berlin wall in 1989.) America and its Western European allies needed West Germany to help them in their Cold War fight against the Soviet Union and Communism. Allied programs to de-Nazify Germany and

American soldiers forced German civilians to look at the dead bodies of concentration camp inmates tortured by the Nazis. To make sure that ordinary Germans could not deny knowledge of what had happened in the camps, the American military authorities often insisted that local citizens be forced to see what had been found in the liberated camps.

hold Nazis accountable for the atrocities of the Holocaust increasingly gave way to the priorities of the Cold War and reconstruction. Many Nazis who were guilty of war crimes went unpunished or were released from prison.

In 1945, Jewish life in Germany lay in ruins. Of the half million Jews who had lived in Germany in 1933, only about fifteen thousand had managed to survive within Germany itself. About 3,500 German Jewish exiles, many of whom were convinced communists, returned to the Soviet Zone of occupation to help build what they believed would be a new and much better socialist Germany. A much larger number of Jews—some 200,000 in all—-fled from Eastern Europe to so-called displaced persons camps in the western zones of occupied Germany. Ironically, Germany under the control of the Allied military authorities had become a much safer place for Jews than other European countries, for example, Poland. Polish Jews who had survived the death camps were often greeted with hatred and even violence when they returned to their towns or villages and attempted to reclaim their homes and property now in the possession of their former neighbors. In July 1946, a Polish mob killed forty-two Jews in the town of Kielce. By the early 1950s, large numbers of European Jewish survivors had emigrated to the United States or to the state of

Israel, which was founded in 1948 after the British withdrawal from Palestine. Great Britain had administered Palestine since the end of World War One.

After the war, the Allies implemented programs designed to eliminate from public office all Nazi officials or other Germans tainted by their direct involvement in the regime. A directive issued by the State Department to the commander in chief of the United States Forces of Occupation on May 10, 1945, describes the original priorities of the Allied military government that ran Germany.

DENAZIFICATION

(a) A Proclamation dissolving the Nazi Party, its formations, affiliated associations and supervised organizations, and all Nazi public institutions which were set up as instruments of Party domination, and prohibiting their revival in any form, should be promulgated by the Control Council. You will assure the prompt effectuation of that policy in your zone and will make every effort to prevent the reconstitution of any such organization in underground, disguised or secret form . . .

(b) The laws purporting to establish the political structure of National Socialism and the basis of the Hitler regime and all laws,

Control Council

The military occupation governing body of Germany. Members were the United States, United Kingdom, Soviet Union, and France

A postwar cartoon suggests that Displaced Persons (D.P.s), many of whom were Holocaust survivors, did not find it easy to leave war-ravaged Europe for a new life in the United States.

decrees and regulations which establish discriminations on grounds of race, nationality, creed or political opinions should be abrogated by the Control Council. You will render them inoperative in your zone.

(c) All members of the Nazi Party who have been more than nominal participants in its activities, all active supporters of Nazism or militarism and all other persons hostile to Allied purposes will be removed and excluded from public office and from positions of importance in quasi-public and private enterprises such as 1) civic, economic, and labor organizations, 2) corporations and other organizations in which the German government or subdivisions have a major financial interest, 3) industry, commerce, agriculture, and finance, 4) education, and 5) the press, publishing houses, and other agencies disseminating news and propaganda. Persons are to be treated as more than nominal participants in Party activities and as active supporters of Nazism or militarism when they have 1) held office or otherwise been active at any level from local to national in the party and its subordinate organizations, or in organizations which further militaristic doctrines, 2) authorized or participated affirmatively in any Nazi crimes, racial persecutions or discriminations, 3) been avowed believers in Nazism or racial and militaristic creeds, or 4) voluntarily given substantial moral or material support or political assistance of any kind to the Nazi Party or Nazi officials and leaders. No such persons shall be retained in any of the categories of employment listed above because of administrative necessity, convenience or expediency...

SUSPECTED WAR CRIMINALS AND SECURITY ARRESTS
(a) You will search out, arrest, and hold, pending receipt by you

German military leaders sign the formal unconditional surrender of all German troops to the Allied powers. The Allies ruled out any possibility of a negotiated peace with Hitler's regime and decided to occupy and govern Germany for an unspecified period of time.

of further instructions as to their disposition, Adolf Hitler, his chief Nazi associates, other war criminals and all persons who have participated in planning or carrying out Nazi enterprises involving or resulting in atrocities or war crimes.

(b) All persons who, if permitted to remain at large would endanger the accomplishment of your objectives will also be arrested and held in custody until trial by an appropriate semi-judicial body to be established by you...

In no event shall any differentiation be made between or special consideration be accorded to persons arrested...upon the basis of wealth or political, industrial, or other rank or position. In your discretion you may make such exceptions as you deem advisable for intelligence or other military reasons...

EDUCATION

...(b) A coordinated system of control over German education and an affirmative program of reorientation will be established designed completely to eliminate Nazi and militaristic doctrines and to encourage the development of democratic ideas.

(c) You will permit the reopening of elementary (Volksschulen), middle (Mittelschulen}, and vocational (Berufsschulen) schools at the earliest possible date after Nazi personnel have been eliminated. Textbooks and curricula which are not free of Nazi and militaristic doctrine shall not be used. The Control Council should devise programs looking toward the reopening of secondary schools, universities, and other institutions of higher learning....

(d) It is not intended that the military government will intervene in questions concerning denominational control of German schools, or in religious instruction in German schools, except insofar as may be necessary to insure that religious instruction and administration of such schools conform to such Allied regulations as are or may be established pertaining to purging of personnel and curricula.

The Nuremberg trials of the major Nazi leaders made a powerful statement that these men would have to answer for the crimes they committed. Yet, Nuremberg also made it easy for many ordinary Germans to see only these top leaders as the guilty parties and not to ask difficult questions about their own role in supporting and promoting the criminal Nazi regime. The Nuremberg trials continued into the late 1940s and resulted in the indictments of lower-level Nazi officials. Francis Biddle was one of the American judges at the Nuremberg trial. In his 1962 memoir, he describes the responses of the defendants to the charges against them.

A lot of unhappiness and damage has been caused by denazification.... Those who are truly guilty of crimes committed in the National Socialist period and in the war should be most severely punished.... But as for the rest we must no longer distinguish between two classes of people in Germany...those who are politically beyond reproach and those who are reproachable.

—Konrad Adenauer, first elected leader of West Germany, in his inaugural speech before the new parliament, September 20, 1949

American and Russian chiefs of staff gathered at a conference in Potsdam, near Berlin, between July 17 and August 2, 1945, to discuss the fate of occupied Germany.

We watched the defendants day after day, these drab men once great, most of them now turning on the Führer who had led them to their brief spasm of violent triumph. A few were still "loyal." Some felt that it was not "correct" to attack a dead man who had been head of the State. Others transferred their guilt to the man who, they said, was alone responsible, from whom, they pleaded, orders came to them that had to be obeyed: theirs but to do or die, they argued; how could there be a conspiracy, a meeting of the minds, when one man's mind commanded all the others?...

Day after day the horrors accumulated—tortures by the Gestapo in France, scientific "experiments" on prisoners who died in agony, the gas chambers, the carefully planned liquidation of the Jews. Hour on hour the twenty-one men in the dock listened, and the shame spread, and steadily washed to the rocks of their loyalty to the man who was responsible for it all. After one day's evidence Hans Fritzsche was physically ill in his cell. And when Hans Frank, the notorious Governor General of Poland, made his cheap, dramatic confession—"a thousand years will pass and still this guilt of Germany will not have been erased"—Schacht observed to [court psychologist Gustav] Gilbert that Göring's united front of loyalty and defiance seemed to have collapsed. After Gisevius had testified, the legend was warped and tarnished.

Speer tried in his testimony to destroy it forever. The Führer principle, he had at last realized, the authoritarian system, was fundamentally wrong. In 1945 when the situation had become hopeless Hitler "attributed the outcome of the war in an increasing degree to the failure of the German people, but he never blamed himself. . . . The German people remained faithful to Adolf Hitler to the end. He knowingly betrayed them."

The new West German state founded in 1949 (the Federal Republic of Germany) realized that it must make some kind of amends to the Jewish survivors of the Holocaust if it wanted to be rehabilitated in the eyes of Western Europe and the United States. In September 1952, the West German chancellor (prime minister) Konrad Adenauer explained in a speech to his political party, the Christian Democratic Union, why Germany should make restitution payments to Israel.

Now I would like to say this to you about the agreement with Israel: It is absolutely true that Germany, the Federal Republic, does not have any legal obligations with regard to the Republic of Israel, but the Federal Republic does have great moral obligations. Even though we, and I am referring here to our circle, did not participate in the atrocities of National Socialism against the Jews, a considerable number of the German people did participate in them, and they not only actively participated, a certain percentage also got rich afterwards from their participation. We cannot ignore this fact. I consider it one of the most noble moral obligations of the German people to do, within their ability, whatever must be done to at least show that they do not agree with what was done to the Jews in the years of National Socialism, even if only by symbolic action. In unanimous resolutions the Bundestag [West German parliament] has repeat-

Jewish Holocaust survivors sailing to Palestine in the late 1940s raise the Zionist flag. The great majority of the eastern European Jews fled to occupied Germany after the war, but they soon moved on, emigrating mainly to Israel or to the United States. By the early 1950s, there were fewer than 15,000 Jews in all of Germany.

The peoples who know that the members of their people are in mass graves remember them, particularly the Jews who were practically forced by Hitler into a consciousness of their own ethnicity. They will never, they can never forget what was done to them; the Germans must never forget what was done by people of their nationality in these shameful years.

—Theodor Heuss, first President of the Federal Republic of Germany, speaking at the dedication of the memorial for the victims of Bergen-Belsen concentration camp, November 1952

edly expressed regret concerning the heinous crimes of the past against the Jews. Whoever speaks must also act. Words are cheap. But words must be followed by actions.

There is also a certain legal basis to the demands of the state of Israel, since it was after all due to measures taken by Germany that Israel had to accommodate so many refugees, especially old people from Germany and from countries that were occupied by Germany at the time; this resulted in serious financial burdens for Israel. It has been proposed that, following a cabinet meeting on Monday morning, I will go to Luxembourg, and in Luxembourg a kind of symbolic declaration will take place between me and the Minister of Foreign Affairs of Israel. This declaration is to express that from now on the past shall be past between the Jews and Germany. The representatives of the large Jewish world organization will also take part in this declaration.

I hope that the cabinet will not make things difficult for me. If the cabinet did cause problems, it would be a foreign policy disaster of the first order. It would not only be a political disaster, it would also strongly impede all our efforts to acquire foreign credit again. Let us be clear that now as before the power of the Jews in the economic sphere is extraordinarily strong, so that this—the term is perhaps a bit overstated—this reconciliation with the Jews is an absolute requirement for the Federal Republic from a moral standpoint and a political standpoint as well as an economic standpoint.

I have intentionally dwelled on this topic in somewhat more detail because I fear that afterwards all kinds of things will be said about this issue in Germany, and there will be difficulties. What I am telling you now does not have to be an absolute truth, but at one time I was told by a leading American authority: If the Federal Government succeeds in reaching this settlement with Israel and with the Jewish world organizations, it will be a political event for the Federal Republic of Germany comparable to the Germany treaty and the agreement on the European Defense Community. Therefore I ask you, if the matter turns out as I hope, and if opposition also arises in our own ranks, nonetheless to reflect on my words and to help people really appreciate that the settlement with the Jews is morally, politically, and economically an absolute necessity.

In the other Germany (the German Democratic Republic, or communist East Germany), the Communist leaders refused to accept any responsibility for the consequences of the Nazis'

crimes, claiming that Communists had always fought against Nazism and had paid a heavy price for their resistance by long years of exile or imprisonment in concentration camps. The Nazis had murdered many Communists, so Communist East Germany felt it had no reason to make amends for Germany's Nazi past. In September 1958, the prime minister of East Germany Otto Grotewohl spelled out the official Communist regime's view at dedication ceremonies for the memorial constructed by the East German government at the site of the Buchenwald concentration camp.

THE IDEA OF THE FALLEN ANTI-FASCISTS LIVES ON

... Today for the first time the bells ring from the tower of the National Memorial, resonating far into the countryside and proclaiming the heroism of the European resistance fighters. They defied the dark, terrible night of Hitler-fascism; they gave their blood and their lives, their joy and their happiness in order to end the cruel fascist slavery. The voices of the dead and the living unite in the sound of the bells to utter a warning cry: Never again fascism and war!...

The anti-fascist fighters who died gave us that mission. Their idea lives; it is risen out of war, misery, and ruins...

THE ANTI-FASCIST RESISTANCE STRUGGLE IS A PEOPLE'S STRUGGLE

... The anti-fascist resistance struggle was and is a people's struggle. It can only lead to success where the peoples rise up resolutely under the leadership of their working class to fight against fascist reaction. The resistance struggle against Hitler-fascism was also organized and led by the working class and their parties.

... Nazi rule in Germany was a fascist dictatorship of the most reactionary circles of German imperialism. Its goal was the establishment of fascist world rule under German leadership. Its method was unrestrained terror and bloody mass murder...

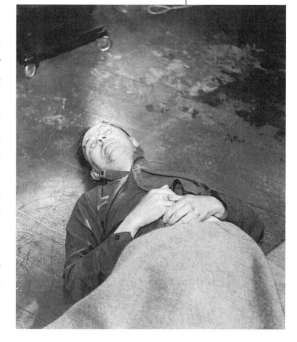

When the German forces surrendered, Heinrich Himmler, leader of the SS and major architect of the Holocaust, tried to evade capture by assuming a false identity. British troops still managed to arrest him, but he committed suicide with a poison capsule before he could be put on trial for his many crimes.

More than 18 million people were deported to the extermination factories, the concentration camps. More than 11 million of them were murdered in the most brutal way. Here on this site, in the Buchenwald concentration camp, more than 56,000 people lost their lives...

We thank first of all the heroic Soviet Union, the courageous sons and daughters of socialism, and the millions of nameless heroes of the anti-fascist resistance movement from many countries in Europe for the victory over this abominable system. They shed their blood and gave their lives to crush Hitler-fascism.

WARNING FOR ALL TIMES
...This memorial shall be a place of friendship with the great Soviet people, who liberated our people and Europe from Hitler-fascism...We call the living to action; we admonish them not to grow weary in the fight against fascism and to continue to lead the people to success for world peace. With the cry: "People of all lands—defend the greatest good of humankind, peace!" this ceremony can become a protest demonstration against the preparation for an imperialistic atomic war, which, especially coming from West Germany today, threatens the German people and humankind.

Hitler-fascism was crushed militarily in 1945, but it was only destroyed at the roots in one part of Germany, in the German Democratic Republic...

Today two German states stand before the world. One has learned from the mistakes of German history. It has learned good and right lessons. It is the German Democratic Republic—a state of peace and socialism.

But the West German state is a refuge of reactionaries in which militarists and fascists have attained power once again; the state's aggressive character is revealed in its reactionary actions...

Fatefully involved in the politics of the NATO alliance, the forces of yesterday stand ready in West Germany to seek revenge for the defeat they suffered and to plunge the people into a new horrible war. Once again they rule the state and the economy; they are raising the youth for a new war, and they control the entire reactionary propaganda industry...

Thus the old fascist system in West Germany is currently becoming "socially acceptable" once again. It is high time to change the situation in West Germany. Threatening clouds darken the light of peace and freedom...We must not allow the world to be plunged again into blood and misery and the people to be forced to the edge of catastrophe. The decision whether the nations follow the path toward peace or whether they steer toward the abyss of a third world war lies in the hands of peace-loving people.

In a secret wartime memo, a German official wrote to Adolf Eichmann's SS department about the deportation of six thousand French Jews to Auschwitz. After Germany's defeat, Eichmann was arrested and placed in an American internment camp, but he managed to escape. In 1950, he fled to Argentina and lived there under an assumed name until May 1960, when Israeli secret service agents arrested him and took him to Israel. This document was later used as evidence in Eichmann's 1961 trial in Jerusalem.

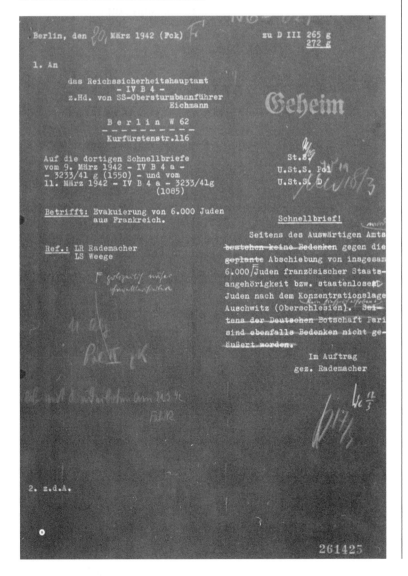

An Israeli court sentences Adolf Eichmann to death in 1961 as he stands behind bulletproof glass. As a high-ranking officer in the SS, Eichmann had organized the deportations of Jews from all over Europe to the extermination camps in Poland. His trial sixteen years after the end of the war reminded Germany and the world that many major Nazi war criminals had still not been brought to justice.

The "negative inheritance" of the Holocaust has become a permanent component of German national identity. Today, the history of the Holocaust is taught in the German school system, and the Nazi era is a common theme in German fiction, films, and television shows. It is difficult for contemporary Germans to think about what it means to be German without at the same time confronting the fact that the Holocaust is an undeniable chapter of German history. In October 2001, Rob Broomby, a British Broadcasting Corporation reporter in Berlin, wrote an article describing the new national Holocaust memorial, designed by the American architect Peter Eisenman, that today covers a large site in the very center of re-united Berlin.

Work has begun in central Berlin on a massive Holocaust memorial, almost 2,000 square metres in size. A large digger has started the process of turning this huge plot of land into a monument to the six million Jews of Europe killed by the Nazis.

The $22m scheme, located just a few hundred metres from the Brandenburg Gate—the symbol of German nationhood—is an enormous gesture of national remorse. The location between the symbolic gate and the bunker where Adolph Hitler died is as important as the design itself. . . .

The idea for a monument predates the fall of the Berlin Wall, though the plot of land was not set aside until 1993. Initial plans for a huge iron plate, measuring 100 metres by 100 metres, and bearing the names of some four-and-a-half million Jews, was vetoed by the then chancellor, Helmut Kohl.

The present design, with its 2,700 concrete pillars of differing heights, was described by the architect, Peter Eisenman, as a waving cornfield. It . . . is set just below street level. The Bundestag president, Wolfgang Thierse, said the beginning of construction work showed an assertion of Germany's historical responsibility. The memorial is expected to be completed by 27 January 2004— the 59th anniversary of the liberation of Auschwitz [the monument was opened in May 2005].

The Memorial to the Murdered Jews of Europe displays 2,711 concrete slabs in a grid pattern on a huge site in the center of Berlin. Visitors can walk through the monument, along pathways between the markers. The changing depth of the pathways and different heights of the concrete slabs are meant to produce unease and confusion.

Timeline

1889
Adolf Hitler is born in Braunau am Inn, Austria

1908–1913
Hitler lives in Vienna

1914–1918
World War I is fought in Europe; Hitler serves on the Western Front

1918
Germans revolt against Kaiser Wilhelm II and proclaim German Republic in Berlin; the kaiser abdicates

1919
Germany signs Versailles Treaty; Hitler joins German Workers' Party in Munich

1920
German Workers' Party issues its program and changes its name to National Socialist German Workers' Party

1921
Nazis found their paramilitary organization, the SA (storm troopers)

1923
French and Belgian troops occupy Ruhr, in western Germany; Hitler attempts to seize power in Bavaria

1924
Hitler is tried for high treason and is sentenced to five years in prison but released before the end of the year

1925
Paul von Hindenburg elected as president of the republic; Hitler's *Mein Kampf* published

1932
Nazis increase their percent of the vote in national elections to 37.3 and become largest single party in the Reichstag (national parliament) with 230 seats

1933
Hitler appointed chancellor; Heinrich Himmler establishes first concentration camp at Dachau; nationwide boycott of Jewish stores; trade unions dissolved; books by "un-German" authors burned in cities across Germany; Germany becomes a one-party state

1934
On the "Night of Long Knives" SS officers murder the SA leadership; Reich President von Hindenburg dies

1935

The League of Nations returns the Saar province to Germany; Nazis introduce conscription and expand the army; Nuremberg Racial Laws ban marriage and sexual relations between Jews and non-Jews

1936

Hitler reoccupies demilitarized Rhineland

1938

Germany annexes Austria; Munich conference results in ethnic-German Sudeten border region of western Czechoslovakia being given to Germany; Kristallnacht takes place

1939

Hitler's army occupies rest of Czechoslovakia; Hitler defeats Poland; euthanasia campaign begins; Polish Jews forced to wear yellow Star of David

1940

German Army invades Denmark and Norway and defeats Netherlands, Belgium, and France; Battle of Britain begins

1941

Germany attacks Yugoslavia and Greece; Hitler invades Soviet Union, but German Army halted before it reaches Moscow; mass shootings of Jews by *Einsatzgruppen*

1942

Systematic mass gassings of Jews begin in Auschwitz-Birkenau; German Sixth Army encircled at Stalingrad

1943

German Sixth Army surrenders at Stalingrad; Jews in Warsaw ghetto stage uprising; Allies land in Sicily; major tank battles fought at Kursk; Soviets recapture Kiev

1944

Germany occupies Hungary; Allies invade France on the Normandy coast; German officers' attempt to kill Hitler and overthrow Nazi regime fails; Soviet

Army liberates Majdanek concentration camp; American and French troops enter Paris

1945

Red Army liberates Auschwitz; American troops enter Buchenwald concentration camp; British troops liberate Bergen-Belsen concentration camp; American and Soviet troops meet at Elbe River; Hitler commits suicide in Berlin bunker; Red Army occupies Berlin; Germany capitulates to Allies

Further Reading

World War I, Weimar, and Hitler's Rise to Power

Allen, William Sheridan. *The Nazi Seizure of Power: The Experience of a Single German Town: 1922–1945*. New York: Franklin Watts, 1984.

Bessel, Richard. *Germany after the First World War*. Oxford, England: Clarendon Press, 1993.

Bridenthal, Renate, Atina Grossmann, and Marion Kaplan, eds. *When Biology Became Destiny: Women in Weimar and Nazi Germany*. New York: Monthly Review Press, 1984.

Coetzee, Frans and Marilyn Shevin-Coetzee. *World War I: A History in Documents*. New York: Oxford University Press, 2002.

Daniel, Ute. *The War from Within: German Working-Class Women in the First World War*. New York: Berg, 1997.

Davis, Belinda J. *Home Fires Burning: Food, Politics, and Everyday Life in World War I Berlin*. Chapel Hill: University of North Carolina Press, 2000.

Fallada, Hans. *Little Man, What Now?* New York: Simon and Schuster, 1933.

Fritzsche, Peter. *Germans into Nazis*. Cambridge, Mass.: Harvard University Press, 1998.

Kaes, Anton, Martin Jay, and Edward Dimendberg, eds. *The Weimar Republic Sourcebook*. Berkeley: University of California Press, 1994.

Kershaw, Ian. *Hitler, 1889–1936: Hubris*. New York: W.W. Norton, 1998.

Kessler, Charles, ed. *Berlin in Lights: The Diaries of Count Harry Kessler (1918–1937)*. New York: Grove, 1999.

Peukert, Detlev J. K. *The Weimar Republic: The Crisis of Classical Modernity*. New York: Hill and Wang, 1992.

Remarque, Erich Maria. *All Quiet on the Western Front*. New York: Ballantine, 1987.

Nazi Dictatorship

Ayçoberry, Pierre. *The Social History of the Third Reich, 1933–1945*. New York: New Press, 1998.

Bessel, Richard, ed. *Life in the Third Reich*. New York: Oxford University Press, 1987.

Burleigh, Michael. *The Third Reich: A New History*. New York: Hill and Wang, 2000.

Crew, David F., ed. *Nazism and German Society, 1933–1945*. New York: Routledge, 1994.

Gellately, Robert. *Backing Hitler: Consent and Coercion in Nazi Germany*. New York: Oxford University Press, 2001.

Gilbert, Martin. *The Dent Atlas of the Holocaust*. London: J.M. Dent, 1993.

Kershaw, Ian. *Hitler, 1936–1945: Nemesis*. New York: W.W. Norton, 2000.

Kershaw, Ian. *Popular Opinion and Political Dissent in the Third Reich: Bavaria 1933–1945*. Oxford: Clarendon, 1983.

Klemperer, Victor. *The Language of the Third Reich, LTI-Lingua Tertii Imperii: A Philologist's Notebook*. New York: Continuum, 2000.

Koonz, Claudia. *Mothers in the Fatherland: Women, the Family and Nazi Politics*. New York: St. Martin's, 1987.

Petropoulos, Jonathan. *Art as Politics in the Third Reich*. Chapel Hill: University of North Carolina Press, 1996.

Peukert, Detlev J. K. *Inside Nazi Germany: Conformity, Opposition, and Racism in Everyday Life*. New Haven, Conn.: Yale University Press, 1987.

Speer, Albert. *Inside the Third Reich: Memoirs*. London: Weidenfeld and Nicolson, 1970.

Stackelberg, Roderick. *Hitler's Germany: Origins, Interpretations, Legacies*. New York: Routledge, 1999.

Taylor, Fred, ed. *The Goebbels Diaries, 1939–1941*. New York : Putnam, 1983.

Taylor, James, and Warren Shaw. *The Third Reich Almanac*. New York: World Almanac, 1987.

Wistrich, Robert S. *Who's Who in Nazi Germany*. New York: Routledge, 1995.

The Racial State

Aly, Götz, Peter Chroust, and Christian Pross, eds. *Cleansing the Fatherland: Nazi Medicine and Racial Hygiene.* Baltimore, Md.: Johns Hopkins University Press, 1994.

Bajohr, Frank. *"Aryanisation" in Hamburg: The Economic Exclusion of Jews and the Confiscation of Their Property in Nazi Germany.* New York: Berghahn, 2001.

Burleigh, Michael, and Wolfgang Wippermann. *The Racial State: Germany 1933–1945.* Cambridge, England: Cambridge University Press, 1991.

Friedländer, Saul. *Nazi Germany and the Jews: The Years of Persecution 1933–1939.* New York: HarperCollins, 1997.

Kater, Michael. *The Twisted Muse: Musicians and their Music in the Third Reich.* New York: Oxford University Press, 1997.

Klemperer, Victor. *I Will Bear Witness: A Diary of the Nazi Years, 1933–1941.* New York: Random House, 1998.

Proctor, Robert N. *Racial Hygiene: Medicine under the Nazis.* Cambridge, Mass.: Harvard University Press, 1988.

Hitler's War

Bartov, Omer. *Hitler's Army: Soldiers, Nazis, and War in the Third Reich.* New York: Oxford University Press, 1991.

Beck, Earl R. *Under the Bombs: The German home Front: 1942–1945.* Lexington: University of Kentucky Press, 1986.

Overy, R. J. *Why the Allies Won.* New York: W.W. Norton, 1997.

Steinert, Marlis G. *Hitler's War and the Germans: Public Mood and Attitude During the Second World War.* Athers: Ohio University Press, 1977.

Rossino, Alexander B. *Hitler Strikes Poland: Blitzkrieg, Ideology, and Atrocity.* Lawrence: University Press of Kansas, 2003.

Wall, Donald W. *Nazi Germany and World War II.* Belmont, Calif.: Wadsworth, 2003.

The Holocaust

Bartov, Omer, ed. *The Holocaust: Origins, Implementation, Aftermath.* New York: Routledge, 2000.

Berenbaum, Michael. *The World Must Know: The History of the Holocaust As Told in the United States Holocaust Memorial Museum.* New York: Little, Brown, 1993.

.Browning, Christopher R. *The Path to Genocide: Essays on Launching the Final Solution.* Cambridge, England: Cambridge University Press, 1992.

Dwork, Deborah. *Children with a Star: Jewish Youth in Nazi Europe.* New Haven, Conn.: Yale University Press, 1991.

Dwork, Deborah, and Robert Jan van Pelt. *Holocaust: A History.* New York: W.W. Norton, 2002.

Hoess, Rudolf. *Commandant of Auschwitz: The Autobiography of Rudolf Hoess.* London: Phoenix, 2000.

Levi, Primo. *Survival in Auschwitz: The Nazi Assault on Humanity.* New York: Touchstone, 1996.

Marrus, Michael R. *The Nuremberg War Crimes Trial, 1945–46: A Documentary History.* Boston: Bedford, 1997.

Roseman, Mark. *A Past in Hiding: Memory and Survival in Nazi Germany.* New York: Henry Holt, 2000.

Websites

Auschwitz-Birkenau Memorial and Museum

www.auschwitz.org.pl

The official website of the Auschwitz-Birkenau memorial provides detailed information on the history of this major Nazi concentration and extermination camp, from its establishment in 1940 to its liberation in January 1945.

Documentation and Cultural Centre of German Sinti and Roma (Gypies)

www.sintiundroma.de/english.html

This permanent exhibition, much of which is available online, documents the treatment of Gypsies at the hands of the Third Reich.

German Propaganda Archive

www.calvin.edu/academic/cas/gpa

Maintained by a professor at Calvin College in Michigan, this archive preserves propaganda speeches, posters, photographs, and other original material covering pre-1933 Germany, the Nazi era (1933*n*45), and the post-1945 East German dictatorship.

The History Place

www.historyplace.com

This website presents detailed chronologies of Hitler's rise to power, World War II, and the Holocaust, as well as concise biographies of major Nazi figures, excerpts from original Nazi documents, and a large number of historical photographs.

Imperial War Museum

www.iwm.org.uk

Covering all aspects of twentieth-century conflict, this British museum's website has a huge digitized collection of images as well as online exhibits.

The Museum of the Great War

www.historial.org/us/home.htm

This museum shows how the Germans, British, French, and Americans perceived and experienced World War I from different vantage points. The website presents a selection of the museum's collection of posters, lithographs, press clippings, objects, uniforms, postcards, books and periodicals, photographs, scrapbooks, and other documents.

The National D-Day Museum

www.ddaymuseum.org

The website of America's World War II museum details U.S. involvement in the war with a rich array of photographs, artifacts, and online exhibits.

Nazi Crimes on Trial

www1.jur.uva.nl/junsv

This website provides a detailed listing and description of post–1945 trials for Nazi war crimes compiled by professors at the Institute of Criminal Law of the University of Amsterdam.

Survivors of the Shoah Visual History Foundation

www.vhf.org

Started by movie director Steven Spielberg, this foundation preserves the testimonies of Holocaust survivors and other witnesses, many of which are available online.

The United States Holocaust Memorial Museum

www.ushmm.org

This comprehensive website of this Washington, D.C., museum includes online exhibits, a multimedia archive, video clips of survivors' testimony, and detailed articles about all aspects of the Holocaust.

Yad Vashem: The Holocaust Martyrs' and Heroes' Remembrance Authority

www.yadvashem.org

The website of the official Israeli Holocaust memorial and museum includes access to a database which Yad Vashem and its partners have recorded the names of half of the six million Jews murdered by the Nazis during the Holocaust.

Text Credits

Main Text

p. 20: Erich Maria Remarque, *All Quiet on the Western Front* (London: Granada, 1977), p. 91.

p. 20–21: Ernst Jünger, "Fire," in *The Weimar Republic Sourcebook*, ed. Anton Kaes, Martin Jay, and Edward Dimendberg (Berkeley: University of California Press, 1994), pp.18–19. © 1994 The Regents of the University of California.

p. 21–22: *Berliner Tageblatt*, May 19,1916, quoted in Ute Daniel, *The War from Within: German Working-Class Women in the First World War* (New York: Berg, 1997), p. 191.

p. 22–24: Kaes, Jay, and Dimendberg, eds., *The Weimar Republic Sourcebook*, p. 46. © 1994 The Regents of the University of California.

p. 24–25: The Treaty of Versailles: The Reparations Clauses, first published in *The Treaty of Peace between the Allied and Associated Powers and Germany* (London: His Majesty's Stationery Office, 1919),

p. 25–26: Paul von Hindenburg, "The Stab in the Back," *Stenographischer Bericht über die öffentlichen Verhandlungen des 75. Untersuchungsausschusses der verfassungsgebenden Nationalversammlung*, testimony delivered on November 18, 1919, trans., vol. 2 (Berlin, 1920), pp.700–1. Reproduced in Kaes, Jay, and Dimendberg, eds., *The Weimar Republic Sourcebook*, pp. 15–16. © 1994 The Regents of the University of California.

p. 26–28: Spartacus Manifesto, November 26, 1918, reproduced in Kaes, Jay, and Dimendberg, eds., *The Weimar Republic Sourcebook*, pp. 37–8. © 1994 The Regents of the University of California.

p. 29: Friedrich Hollaender, lyrics in translation in the liner notes for the CD *Ute Lemper. Berlin Cabaret Songs*, Matrix Ensemble Robert Ziegler, Decca Music Group.

p. 30-31: Elsa Herrmann, *So ist die neue Frau* (This is the New Woman, Hellerau: Avalon Verlag, 1929), pp. 32–43 in Kaes, Jay, and Dimendberg, eds., *The Weimar Republic Sourcebook*, Don Reneau, trans., pp. 206–8. © 1994 The Regents of the University of California.

p. 31–32: Siegfried Kracauer, *The Mass Ornament: Weimar Essays* (Cambridge, Mass.: Harvard University Press, 1995), pp. 292, 299–300. Reprinted by permission of the publisher from, THE MASS ORNAMENT: WEIMAR ESSAYS

by Siegfried Kracauer, translated and edited by Thomas Y. Levin, pp. 292, 299-300, Cambridge, Mass.: Harvard University Press, Copyright © 1995 by the President and Fellows of Harvard College.

p. 32–33: "Textile Workers: My Workday, My Weekend," in *Mein Arbeitstag. Mein Wochenende. 150 Berichte von Textilarbeiterinenn*, ed. Deutscher Textilarbeiterverband (Berlin: Textilpraxis Verlag, 1930), in Kaes, Jay, and Dimendberg, eds., *The Weimar Republic Sourcebook*, p. 208.

p. 34–35: Moritz Julius Bonn, *Wandering Scholar* (New York: John Day, 1948), pp. 286–90. In Fritz K. Ringer, ed., *The German Inflation of 1923* (New York: Oxford University Press, 1969), pp. 99–103.

p. 35–37: Hans Fallada, *Little Man, What Now?* (New York: Simon and Schuster, 1933), pp. 368–69. Reproduced with the permission of Aufbau-Verlag GmbH, Berlin.

p. 41–42: J. Noakes and G. Pridham, eds., *Nazism: A History in Documents and Eyewitness Accounts 1919–1945*, vol. 1 (New York: Schocken, 1983), pp. 12–14.

p. 42: "Document 3. The 25 Points of the Nazi Party Programme," in Frank McDonough, *Hitler and the Rise of the Nazi Party* (London: Pearson, 2003), p. 104.

p. 42–44: Adolf Hitler, *Mein Kampf* trans. Ralph Mannheim (London: Hutchinson, 1984), pp. 426–28. From *Mein Kampf* by Adolf Hitler, published by Pimlico. Reprinted by permission of The Random House Group Ltd.

p. 44: Kurt Ludecke, *I Knew Hitler: The Story of a Nazi Who Escaped the Blood Purge* (London: Jarrolds, 1938), pp. 699–702.

p. 44–46: Louis L. Snyder, ed., *Hitler's Third Reich. A Documentary History* (Chicago: Nelson-Hall, 1991), p. 41.

p. 46: William Sheridan Allen, ed., *The Infancy of Nazism: The Memoirs of Ex-Gauleiter Albert Krebs, 1923–1933* (New York: New Viewpoints, 1976), p. 42.

p. 47–48: Benjamin C. Sax and Dieter Kunz, eds., *Inside Hitler's Germany. A Documentary History of Life in the Third Reich* (Lexington, Mass.: D.C. Heath, 1992), pp. 98–100. © 1992 by Houghton Mifflin Company.

p. 48–49: Simon Taylor, *Germany 1918–1933: Revolution, Counter-Revolution, and the Rise of Hitler* (London: Duckworth, 1983), pp. 83–84.

p. 49–50: Taylor, *Germany 1918–1933*, p. 85.

p. 50–52: Monika Richarz, ed., *Jewish Life in Germany: Memoirs from Three Centuries* (Bloomington: Indiana University Press, 1991), pp. 302–3.

p. 52–53: Noakes and Pridham, *Nazism*, vol. 1, pp. 53–54.

p. 53–55: "A Violent Complement to the Legal Revolution," in Sax and Kuntz, eds., *Inside Hitler's Germany*, pp. 138–39. © 1992 by Houghton Mifflin Company.

p. 55–56: Noakes and Pridham, *Nazism*, vol. 1, pp. 167–68.

p. 56–57: Albert Speer, *Inside the Third Reich: Memoirs* (London: Weidenfeld and Nicolson, 1970), pp. 51–53.

p. 70–72: Louis L. Snyder, ed., *Hitler's Third Reich: A Documentary History* (Chicago: Nelson-Hall, 1991), pp. 211–14.

p. 72–73: "Resolution of a Municipal Council in the Bernkastel District, August 13, 1935," in Benjamin Sax and Dieter Kunz, eds., *Inside Hitler's Germany. A Documentary History of Life in the Third Reich* (Lexington, Mass.: D.C. Heath, 1992), p. 409.

p. 73–74: J. Noakes and G. Pridham, *Nazism 1919–1945. Volume 2. State, Economy and Society: 1933–1939. A Documentary Reader* (Exeter: University of Exeter Press, 2000), p. 589–91.

p. 74–75: Hans Massaquoi, *Destined to Witness: Growing up Black in Nazi Germany* (New York: William Morrow, 1999), p. 46–8. COPYRIGHT © 2000 BY HANS J. MASSAQUOI. Reprinted by permission of Harper Collins Publishers.

p. 75–76: Michael Burleigh and Wolfgang Wippermann, *The Racial State: Germany 1933–1945* (New York; Cambridge University Press, 1991), pp. 120–21

p. 76–78: Burleigh and Wippermann, *The Racial State*, pp. 192–93.

p. 78–79: United States Holocaust Memorial and Museum, www.ushmm.org/wlc/en/index.php?ModuleId=10005261.

p. 79–80: Louis L. Snyder, ed., *Hitler's Third Reich: A Documentary History* (Chicago: Nelson-Hall, 1991), pp. 305–7.

p. 80–82: *The New York Times*, November 11, 1938, in Snyder, *Hitler's Third Reich*, pp. 299–301.

p. 82–84: Hans Berger, "Remembrances of Kristallnacht and My Experiences in the Concentration Camp Buchenwald, manuscript dated Brussels, January 15, 1939" in Monika Richarz, ed., *Jewish Life in Germany: Memoirs from Three Centuries* (Bloomington: Indiana University Press, 1991), pp. 386–96.

p. 84–86: Olga Levy Drucker, *Kindertransport* (New York: Henry Holt, 1992), pp. 37–40. Excerpt from KINDERTRANSPORT by Olga Levy Drucker, © 1992 by Olga Levy Drucker. Reprinted by permission of Henry Holt and Company, LLC.

p. 86–87: Max O. Korman, "The Ill-Fated Steamship *St. Louis*," in *Hitler's Exiles: Personal Stories of the Flight from Nazi Germany to America* ed. Mark M. Anderson (New York: New Press, 1998), pp. 187–91. Reprinted by permission of The New Press. www.thenewpress.com.

p. 87–88: *Reichsgesetzblatt*, 1933, vol. 1, p. 529, in *The Nazi Germany Sourcebook: An Anthology of Texts*, ed. Roderick Stackelberg and Sally A. Winkle (New York: Routledge, 2002), pp. 154–55. Copyright © 2002. Reproduced by permission of Routledge/Taylor & Francis Group, LLC.

p. 88–89: Noakes and Pridham, *Nazism*, vol. 2, p. 255.

p. 89–90: Alfons Heck, *The Burden of Hitler's Legacy* (Frederick, Colo.: Renaissance House, 1988), pp. 57–58.

p. 90–92: Melita Maschmann, *Account Rendered: A Dossier on My Former Self*, trans. Geoffrey Strachan (London: Abelard-Schumann, 1964), pp. 12, 16, 18–19, 20, 22–23.

p. 92–93: Noakes and Pridham, *Nazism*, vol. 2, p. 439.

p. 93–95: Office of the U.S. Chief of Counsel for Prosecution of Axis Criminality, *Nazi Conspiracy and Aggression*, vol. 4 (Washington, D.C.: Government Printing Office, 1946), pp. 624–34. In Stackelberg and Winkle, eds., *The Nazi Germany Sourcebook*, p. 205–7. Copyright © 2002. Reproduced by permission of Routledge/Taylor & Francis Group, LLC.

p. 95–97: Lina Haag, *Eine Handvoll Staub: Widerstand einer Frau 1933–1945* (1947). Reprint (Frankfurt: Fischer Taschenbuch Verlag, 1995), pp. 107, 111–13, 117–19. Sally Winkle, trans., in Stackelberg and Winkle, *The Nazi Germany Sourcebook*, pp. 146–49. Copyright © 2002. Reproduced by permission of Routledge/Taylor & Francis Group, LLC.

p. 101: "Reflections on the Treatment of the Peoples of Alien Races in the East," in *Witness to the Holocaust*, ed. Michael Berenbaum (New York: HarperCollins, 1997), pp. 75–76.

p. 102: J. Noakes and G. Pridham, *Nazism: 1919–1945, Volume 3: Foreign Policy, War and Racial Extermination: A Documentary Reader* Exeter: University of Exeter Press, p. 904.

p. 102–103: *The War in Pictures* (London: Odhams Press, 1940), pp. 296, 298, 300.

p. 103–104: Stephen E. Ambrose, *American Heritage New History of World War II* (New York: Viking, 1997), p. 94.

p. 104–106: Norman Cameron and R. H. Stevens, trans., *Hitler's Secret Conversations, 1941–1944* (New York: Octagon, 1976), pp. 28–30, 56–57, 343–45.

p. 106–107: Office of the U.S. Chief of Counsel for Prosecution of Axis Criminality, *Nazi Conspiracy and Aggression*, vol. 8 (Washington, D.C.: Government Printing Office, 1946), pp. 585–87. In Roderick Stackelberg and Sally A. Winkle, eds., *The Nazi Germany Sourcebook: An Anthology of Texts* (New York: Routledge, 2002). Copyright © 2002. Reproduced by permission of Routledge/Taylor & Francis Group, LLC.

p. 107–108: War letters of the second World War, www.medienberatung.tu-berlin.de/cls/Feldpost/ english/index.html

p. 108–109: *German Crimes in Poland*, Volumes 1–2 (Warsaw, 1946), pp. 268–69, 292. In D. G. Williamson, *The Third Reich* (Harlow, England: Longman, 1982), p. 92.

p. 109: Charles Burdick and Hans-Adolf Jacobsen, eds., *The Halder War Diary, 1939–1942* (Novato, Calif.: Presidio, 1988), p. 506.

p. 109–110: Noakes and Pridham *Nazism*, vol. 3, p. 827.

p. 110–111: www.historyplace.com/worldwar2/timeline/germany-declares.htm

p. 111–112: Louis L. Snyder, ed., *Hitler's Third Reich: A Documentary History* (Chicago: Nelson-Hall, 1991), pp. 456–59.

p. 112–113: Franz Schneider and Charles Gullans, trans., *Last Letters from Stalingrad*, (New York: New American Library, 1961), pp. 46–47, 37–38, 50–51.

p. 113–114: Ulrich Herbert, *A History of Foreign Labor in Germany, 1880–1980: Seasonal Workers/Forced Laborers/Guest Workers*, (Ann Arbor: University of Michigan Press, 1990), p. 149.

p. 114–115: Herbert, *A History of Foreign Labor in Germany, 1880–1980*, p. 157.

p. 115–116: Inge Scholl, *Students against Tyranny: The Resistance of the White Rose, Munich, 1942–1943*, trans. Arthur R. Schultz (Middletown, Conn.: Wesleyan University Press, 1970), pp. 89–90. © 1970 by Inge Scholl. Reprinted with permission of Wesleyan University Press

p. 116–118: Noakes & Pridham, *Nazism*, vol. 3, pp. 870–71.

p. 118: Jeremy Noakes, ed. *Nazism: 1919–1945, Volume 4: The German Home Front in World War II: A Documentary Reader* (Exeter: University of Exeter Press, 1998).

p. 118–119: Johannes Steinhoff, Peter Pechel, and Dennis Showalter, *Voices from the Third Reich: An Oral History* (Washington, D.C.: Regnery Gateway, 1989), pp. 215–16.

p. 119: Noakes & Pridham, *Nazism*, vol. 4, pp. 557–58.

p. 122–123: Adolf Hitler, speech to the Reichstag, January 30, 1939, www.historyplace.com/worldwar2/holocaust/h-threat.htm.

p. 123–124: J. Noakes and G. Pridham, *Nazism*, vol. 3 (New York: Schocken, 1983), pp. 1,024–25.

p. 124–125: Victor Klemperer, *I Will Bear Witness, 1933–1941: A Diary of the Nazi Years* (New York: Modern Library, 1999), pp. 433–4.

p. 125–127: Dina Pronicheva, "A Survivor's Eyewitness Account," www.historyplace.com/worldwar2/holocaust/h-b-yar.htm.

p. 127–129: Noakes and Pridham, *Nazism*, vol. 3, pp. 460–62.

p. 129–131: Weiss Fritzshallm, Fritzie, interview, United States Holocaust Memorial Museum Collections, 1990.

p. 131–132: Stern, Bart, interview, United States Holocaust Memorial Museum Collections, 1992.

p. 132–134: "Deathwatch at Belzec: Kurt Gerstein's Deposition" English translation in Lucy S. Dawidowicz, ed., *A Holocaust Reader* (West Orange, N.J.: Behrman House, 1976), pp. 106–8. © Behrman House, Inc., reprinted with permission www.behrmanhouse.com.

p. 134–135: Joanna Bourke, *The Second World War: A People's History* (New York: Oxford University Press, 2001), p. 147.

p. 135: United States Holocaust Memorial and Museum, Washington, D.C., www.ushmm.org/wlc/en/index.php?ModuleId=10005261.

p. 135–137: Varian Fry, *Surrender on Demand* (Boulder, Colo.: Johnson Books, 1997), pp. 186–89.

p. 137–138: Elisabeth Freund, "Waiting," in *Hitler's Exiles: Personal Stories of the Flight from Nazi Germany to America*, ed. Mark M. Anderson (New York: New Press, 1998), pp. 120–28. Reprinted by permission of The New Press. www.thenewpress.com.

p. 139–140: "The Last Letter from Mordecai Anielewicz, Warsaw Ghetto Revolt Commander, April 23, 1943" in *A Holocaust Reader: From Ideology to Annihilation*, ed. Rita Botwinick (Upper Saddle River, N.J.: Prentice Hall, 1998), pp. 191–92.

p. 140–141: Anne Michaels, *Fugitive Pieces* (New York: Vintage, 1996), pp. 213–14.

p. 145–147: U.S. Department of State Publication 9446, *Documents on Germany 1944–1985* (Washington, D.C.: Government Printing Office, 1985), pp. 15–23.

p. 147–149: Francis Biddle, *In Brief Authority* (Garden City, N.Y.: Doubleday, 1962), pp. 424–46, in *The Nuremberg War Crimes Trial 1945–1946: A Documentary History*, ed. Michael R.

Marrus (New York: Bedford, 1997), pp. 77–78. From IN BRIEF AUTHORITY by Francis Biddle, copyright © 1962 by Francis Biddle. Used by permission of Doubleday, a division of Random House, Inc.

p. 149–150: Konrad Adenauer, *Reden 1917–1967: Eine Auswahl*, ed. Hans-Peter Schwarz (Stuttgart: Deutsche Verlags-Anstalt, 1975), pp. 266–67. Sally Winkle, trans., in *The Nazi Germany Sourcebook: An Anthology of Texts*, ed. Roderick Stackelberg and Sally A. Winkle (New York: Routledge, 2002), pp. 400–1. Copyright © 2002. Reproduced by permission of Routledge/Taylor & Francis Group, LLC.

p. 150–151: Otto Grotewohl, *Kampf um die einige Deutsche Demokratische Republik. Reden und Aufsatze*, vol. 6 (Berlin: Dietz Verlag, 1964), pp. 7–14. Sally Winkle, trans., in Stackelberg and Winkle, *The Nazi Germany Sourcebook*, pp. 404–8. Copyright © 2002. Reproduced by permission of Routledge/Taylor & Francis Group, LLC.

p. 154–155: BBC News, Wednesday, 31 October, 2001, *http://news.bbc.co.uk/2/bi/europe/1629856.stm.*

Sidebars

p. 32: Kaes, Jay, and Dimendberg, eds., *The Weimar Republic Sourcebook*, p. 623.

p. 41: Adolf Hitler, *Mein Kampf*, trans. Ralph Mannkeim (London: Hutchinson, 1969), p. 442.

p. 42: Ian Kershaw, *Hitler*, (New York: Longman, 1991), p. 51.

p. 48: Charles Kessler, ed. and trans., *Berlin in Lights: The Diaries of Count Harry Kessler (1918–1937)* (New York: Grove, 1999), p. 396.

p. 52: J. Noakes and G. Pridham, *Nazism: A History in Documents and Eyewitness Accounts 1919–1945*, vol. 1 (New York: Schocken, 1983), pp. 66–7.

p. 54: Noakes and Pridham, vol. 1, Document 46, p. 116.

p. 71: Victor Klemperer, *I Will Bear Witness, 1933–1941: A Diary of the Nazi Years* (New York: Modern Library, 1999), p. 258.

p. 76: Guenter Lewy, *The Nazi Persecution of the Gypsies* (New York: Oxford University Press, 2000), p. 50.

p. 83: Michael Berenbaum, *The World Must Know: The History of the Holocaust As Told in the United States Holocaust Memorial Museum* (New York: Little, Brown, 1993), p. 54.

p. 87: United States Holocaust Memorial Museum, 1999 Oral History Interview with Ernst G.Heppner, www.ushmm.org/lcmedia/viewer/ wlc/testimony.php?RefId=EHF1001M.

p. 97: Noakes and Pridham, vol. 2, Document 373, p. 310.

p. 110: Louis P. Lochner, ed. and trans. *The Goebbels Diaries* (New York: Eagle Books 1948), p. 50.p. 127: Noakes and Pridham, vol. 3, Document 784, p. 1066.

p. 132: Primo Levi, *Survival in Auschwitz: The Nazi Assault on Humanity* (New York: Collier Books, 1961), p. 117.

p. 137: United States Holocaust Memorial Museum, 1990 Oral History Interview with Liny Pajgin Yollick, www.ushmm.org/lcmedia/viewer/ wlc/testimony.php?RefId=LYE0276F

p. 147: Stackelberg and Winkle, eds, *The Nazi Germany Sourcebook* Document 7.5, p. 397.

p. 150: Stackelberg and Winkle, eds, *The Nazi Germany Sourcebook* Document 7.7, p. 402.

Picture Credits

Author's Collection: 35; Bauhaus-Archiv, Berlin / Lucia Moholy, Photographer: 19; Bavarian State Library, Munich: 45, 57, 62 (top and bottom), 65 (top); © Berlin Tourism www.berlin-tourism-information-de: 155; Courtesy of the Blechner family, London: 86; BPK Berlin: 22, 55; BPK Berlin. Photo: Joseph Schorer: 10; Bundesarchiv Bild 101I-287-0872-28A: 108; Bundesarchiv Bild 102-00104: 33; Deutsches Historisches Museum: 27, 37, 53, 54, 66 (top), 70, 79, 81, 89, 90, 114; Courtesy of the Franklin D. Roosevelt Library Digital Archives: 117, 146; Image provided by the German Propaganda Archive (http://www.calvin.edu/cas/gpa/): 61 (top), 64; Historical Archives Krupp, Essen: 23; GE 758, Poster Collection, Hoover Institution Archives: 24; GE 899, Poster Collection, Hoover Institution Archives: 51; © IMAGNO: 105; © IMAGNO / Austrian Archives: 92; © IMAGNO / Thomas Sessler Verlag: 40, 43, 46; By Permission of the Trustees of the Imperial War Museum, London: IWM BU 6738: 151, IWM BU 8684: 119, IWM COL 119: 13, IWM D 1568: 104, IWM GER 18: 101, IWM HU 39714: 111, IWM HU 75533: 103, IWM MH 4919: 38, IWM Q 110886: 26, IWM Q 126: 20, IWM Q 65860: 61 (bottom), IWM Q 81763: 16; Landesarchiv Berlin A Rep. 358-02 Nr. 115898, Bl. 44, picture 1: 78; © Landeshauptatadt Munchen Stadtarchiv: 60; Library of Congress,

Humanities and Social Sciences Division: 142; Library of Congress, Prints and Photographs Division: 91; "Devoir de Mémoire" Donated by: Musee de la Poche Royan, 1940-1945 Le Gua, France: 102; Museum fur Kunst Gewerbe Hamburg: 28, 65(bottom); NARA NWDNS 242 HLB 3609 25: 97; NARA 208-AA-328-HH-13: 109; NARA 208-PP-10A-2: 98; NARA 242-GAP-286B-4: 107; NARA NWDNS-111-SC-203416: 120; NARA NWDNS-111-SC-207193: 144; NARA NWDNS-44-PA-2415: 116; NARA NWDNS-44-PA-85: 112; General Research Division, The New York Public Library, Astor, Lenox and Tilden Foundations: 42; Netherlands Institute for War Documentation: 80; March Chagall, Purim, Philadelphia Museum of Art: The Louis E. Stern Collection, 1963 / © 2005 Artists Rights Society (ARS), New York / ADAGP, Paris: 74; Photofestnyc.com: 31; U. S. Army, courtesy Harry S. Truman Library: 148; USHMM: 63, 131; USHMM, courtesy of Bezirkskrankenhaus Kaufbeuren: 77; USHMM, courtesy of Alex Knobler: 149; USHMM, courtesy of American Jewish Joint Distribution Committee: 82; USHMM, courtesy of Archiwum Dokumentacji Mechanicznej: 134; USHMM, courtesy of Charles Rennie: 67 (bottom); USHMM, courtesy of Daniel Wellner: 125; USHMM, courtesy of Estelle Bechoefer: Cover; USHMM, courtesy of Fritz Gluckstein:

124; USHMM, courtesy George J. Wittenstein, M.D. (photographer): 115; USHMM, courtesy of Hans Pauli: 71; USHMM, courtesy of Israel Government Press Office: 154; USHMM, courtesy of Jack J. Silverstein: 72; USHMM, courtesy of James Blevins: 67 (top); USHMM, courtesy of KZ Gedenkstaette Dachau: 95; USHMM, courtesy of Library of Congress: 94, 126; USHMM, Courtesy of Marion Davy: 75; USHMM, courtesy of Michael O'Hara: 58; USHMM, courtesy of Museum of the Great Patriotic War: 139; USHMM, courtesy of National Archives: 68, 96, 123, 132, 141, 153; USHMM, courtesy of Norbert Wollheim: 145; USHMM, courtesy of Oesterreichisches Institut fuer Zeitgeschichte Bildarchiv: 85; USHMM, courtesy of Richard Freimark: 2, 3; USHMM, courtesy of Sharon Muller: 140; USHMM, courtesy of Walter Meyerhof: 136, 137; USHMM, courtesy of Yad Vashem: 130; USHMM, courtesy of Zydowski Instytut Historyczny Instytut Naukowo-Badawczy: 128; The views or opinions expressed in this book and the context in which the images are used, do not necessarily reflect the views or policy of, nor imply approval or endorsement by, The United States Holocaust Memorial Museum; Photo: The Wiener Library: 66 (bottom), 73

Index

Acknowledgments

I owe a special debt of gratitude to Bob Moeller. At every stage of the book's development, Bob has been extremely generous with his time and insight, providing detailed, perceptive, and invaluable comments and suggestions. I want also to thank my editors at Oxford University Press, Nancy Toff and Nancy Hirsch, who have shepherded this book from the first step of its original conception through to the final production with admirable efficiency. I am, finally, very grateful to my wife, Sara, whose perspective and experience as an eighth-grade social studies teacher has deeply influenced the way this book is organized and written.

About the Author

David F. Crew is professor of history at the University of Texas at Austin. He has also taught at Columbia University and at Cambridge University in England. At the University of Texas, he has been a faculty member of the Normandy Scholar Program—an honors program on the history of World War II—since 1993. In 2002–2003, he was president of the Conference Group on Central European History of the American Historical Association. He is the author of books on nineteenth-century Germany and on the Weimar Republic. He also edited the reader *Nazism and German Society, 1933–1945*.